FRAMING PHOTOGRAPHY
BY
ALLAN R. LAMB, CPF

About the Author

Allan R. Lamb has been in photography since obtaining his B.A. degree in Technology Education, Western Washington State University in 1965, after which he continued advanced study at Ohio University under Clarence White, Jr.. As part of his education, he taught photography for five years. He received his Air Force commission in 1967 and for over twenty years managed Federal photographic programs and organizations until his retirement in 1987. He was chosen Junior Officer of the Year 1974 and decorated for his work in developing new facilities and organizations in Europe, Korea and the United States. He has functioned as a nationally recognized picture framing instructor for the Professional Picture Framers Association (PPFA), Crescent Cardboard Company and Decor Magazine. Allan was president of the Washington State chapter of PPFA for three years and national PPFA competition judge.

He is a founding member of The Guild Of Fine Art Care & Framing Research Project Committee and the Northwest Coalition of the Professional Framers. Allan has actively studied historic photographic processes and cameras in Europe and the United States. His collection of photographic paraphernalia has been used in many of the illustration of this book.

FRAMING PHOTOGRAPHY

VOLUME 6
OF THE
LIBRARY OF PROFESSIONAL PICTURE FRAMING
BY
ALLAN R. LAMB, CPF

COLUMBA PUBLISHING CO. INC.
AKRON, OHIO 44313

LIBRARY OF PROFESSIONAL PICTURE FRAMING
Volume Six
Framing Photography
by Allan Lamb, CPF

Published by Columba Publishing Co. Inc.
Akron, Ohio USA
Copyright Allan R. Lamb 1999, 1996
All rights reserved: International and Domestic
Second Edition, Revised 1999
Printed in the United States of America
ISBN 0-938655-05-1

Editors:
   Vivian Carli Kistler
   Carli Kistler Miller
   Sheri Leigh Galat
Contributing writers:
   Vivian Carli Kistler
   Paul MacFarland
Illustrations:
   Kelly Ross
   Allan Lamb
   Carli Kistler Miller
Photography:
Photography by Allan R. Lamb
except pages
27, 38 & 46 by Barbara Schlueter
44 by Nannette Bedway.

10 9 8 7 6 5 4 3 2

Translation or reproduction of any part of this work, beyond that permitted by the International Copyright Act, without the permission of the copyright owner, is unlawful. Please request permission or further information from the Permissions Department, Columba Publishing Co. 2003 West Market St., Akron, OH 44313.
Telephone: 330.836.2619 / fax 330.836.9659

The information contained in this manual was obtained from the most competent sources and is believed to be reliable. The suggestions are offered in good faith, but without guarantee, because methods of persons are beyond our control. We recommend the user determine, for her/his own purposes, the suitability of all materials and methods suggested. Columba Publishing Co., Inc. and Allan Lamb disclaim all responsibility for loss or damage resulting from the use the information furnished within.

Dedicated to
my Mother,
Ethel L. Lamb

Acknowledgments

Special thanks to Paul J. "Jerry" Wildman, CPF, Wildman's Northwest Pacific Art and Frame, for allowing me to use examples from his collection of old photographic images and for helping me work out many of the book's concepts.

Special thanks to Paul Miller, CPF, Raindrops Gallery, for his input and assistance with the many ideas of this book.

Thanks to the following framers and companies for providing information and encouraging the development of education in the picture framing industry.

Steve Albin, Albin Products, Inc.
Artisan Frame & Moulding
Benson Studio
Roy Carter, CPF
Crescent Cardboard Co.
George Eastman House
John M. Ferens, CPF
Paul Frederick, CPF
Larson•Juhl
Vivian Kistler, CPF, GCF
Lineco, Inc.
Paul MacFarland, CPF
Robert Mayfield, CPF
William P. Parker, CPF
Chris Paschke, CPF
Professional Picture Framers' Association
Hugh Phibbs
Rochester Institute of Technology
Jeff Wanee, CPF

Credits

The following trademarks appear in this book:

Agfa, Division of Bayer, Inc.
EaselMate, Albin Products
Ektacolor, Kodachrome & Kodacolor, Eastman Kodak Co.
EverColor, EverColor Corporation
Filmoplast P90, Filmolux, USA, Inc.
Frame Sealing Tape, Lineco, Inc.
Fujicolor, Fuji Photo Film, USA, Inc.
Ilfochrome Classic, Ilford Photo
Polaroid, Polaroid Corporation
UltraStable, Charles Berger
Tyvek & Mylar, Dupont
Ivory Flakes, Proctor & Gamble
*Rag Mat, Archival PhotoRag Board,
Perfect Mount Board & Perfect Mount Film,*
Crescent Cardboard, Inc.
Sureguard Pro-Tecta-Cote Matte Spray, McDonald
X-Acto, Hunt Manufacturing Co.
Zen Paste & Insta Hinges, Archival Products, LA

Contents

1. **Framing Photography** — 9
   - History of Photography — 10
   - Time Line — 12
   - Early Presentation Techniques/Methods — 14
   - Photo Albums — 16
   - Spray Coatings — 17
   - Identification Chart — 18
   - Mat & Mount Boards — 20

2. **Types of Photographic Processes**
   - *in Alphabetical Order* — 21
   - Albumen — 21
   - Ambrotype — 23
   - Calotype (Talbotype) — 25
   - Carbon Print Process — 26
   - Chromogenic Prints
     (Kodacolor, Ektacolor,
     Konica, Agfa, Fujicolor) — 27
   - Computer Generated Images — 28
   - Crayon Print — 30
   - Cyanotype (Blueprint Process) — 31
   - Daguerreotype — 32
   - Dye Transfer — 34
   - EverColor — 35
   - Gaslight Paper — 36
   - Gum or Bichromate Prints
     (Gum Dichromate) — 37
   - Ilfochrome Classic (Cibachrome) — 38
   - Ivorytype — 39
   - Matt Collodion Printing-Out Paper (POP) — 40
   - Oil Pigment — 41
   - Photogravure — 42
   - Platinum Print (Platinotype) — 43
   - Polaroid — 44
   - Salted Paper Print — 45
   - Silver Developing-Out Gelatin Print — 46
   - Tintype (Ferrotype or Melainotype) — 47
   - UltraStable Permanent Color — 48

3. **Conservation Methods** — 49
   - Hinges — 52
   - Corner Mounts & Edge Mounts — 55
   - Sink Mats — 56

4. **Mounting Methods** — 57
   - Dry Mounting — 57
   - Pressure-Sensitive Mounting — 60
   - Wet Mounting — 62
   - Spray Mounting — 63
   - Static Mounting — 64

5. **Framing Projects** — 65
   - Sink Mat Built Around Photographs
     & Folders — 65
   - Case Mounted Photograph — 66
   - Display Case for a Photographic Album — 67
   - Building a Glass Box with an Easel
     for a Card Photograph — 68
   - Union or Moroccan Case — 70
   - Carte-de-Visite with a Civil War Stamp — 71
   - Card Photograph & its Original Frame — 72
   - Framing Two Moroccan Cases — 73
   - Hinged-cover Door Frame — 74
   - Card Photograph in a Hinged-Door Frame — 75
   - Uncased Ambrotype, Tintype or
     Daguerreotype in a Preserver — 76
   - Table-top Display Case — 77
   - Platform Easel — 78
   - Float Mounting a Card Photograph — 79
   - Multiple Photographs — 81
   - Mounting a Photograph in a Shadowbox
     with a Three-Dimensional Object — 82
   - Card with Oval Photo — 83
   - A Hand Oil-Colored Copy of an Early
     Photograph — 84
   - Large Tintype with its Original Mat — 85
   - Framing a Convex Print — 86

6. **Frequently Asked Questions** — 87

Appendix
   - Photographic Sizes — 88

Glossary — 90

Index — 94

Chapter 1
Framing Photography

Photography has been around since the early 19th century. As a family record as well as an art form, photography is valuable to both museums and individuals.

Although the basic concept of the photographic process has not changed much since the 1840s, the materials and methods to make photographs have changed greatly. Some photographic emulsions were not as stable as others and even today the materials may not offer the permanence people expect. Photographs do not last indefinitely.

Valuable and irreplaceable images should be copied before framing. By understanding the different types of photographs, the proper framing method can be used to prolong the life of the image.

Display in the home or office of some photographic emulsions will reduce the life of the photograph through fading or chemical change. Most color is very unstable and will fade within a few years even if it is kept in the dark. However, not all color emulsions will fade at the same rate: it depends on the manufacturer, the process and the darkroom techniques of the lab. Serious collectors have been known to seal a color photograph in a lightproof container, to keep the photograph cool, dry and dark.

Unfortunately, like lithographs or other forms of art, framing and display will shorten the life of the photograph. Even black and white images are affected by light, heat, humidity and air contamination. Many of the photographic images that were on continuous display during the 1800s do not exist today because of excessive exposure to the elements of light, heat, contaminants and moisture. If treated with care, a properly processed black and white print will outlast the owner by many years.

Photographic images are the result of chemical reactions. Some of these reactions are constantly active. In fact, a completion of the chemical reaction may result in a lost image. Valuable pieces should not be on continuous display.

The purpose of this book is to assist in identifying the type of photograph and recommend suitable framing procedures.

Before framing:
- Find out when it was taken to help identify the emulsion.
- Look for damage such as:
    - gouges or rips in the surface
    - stains and fading
    - brittleness of the substrate

Tools for identification process:
- white cotton gloves
- 8 to 10x loupe or reading glass
- 30x lighted magnifier
- magnet

White gloves should always be worn when handling photographs. They are available at photography supply stores. The loupe and magnifier are used to inspect the photographic surface for identification and damage assessment. The magnet is used for identification of some early photographic products, such as the tintype.

The best way to preserve an image is to have a copy made and frame the copy while storing the original in a dark, dry place. However, owners of original pieces often want to display them. Chapter 5 contains many framing ideas for both antique and modern photographs.

The purpose of this book is to assist in identifying the type of photograph and recommend suitable framing procedures.

History of Photography

Initially, photography was not an art for the common person. Although photography was to become a medium used by all levels of income, the original works were done by wealthy scientists or landowners. Photography was invented around 1826 by Nicephore Niepce. His images were made on pewter, silver and glass and he called this the heliographic process.

Shortly before Niepce's death in 1833, he was joined in partnership by another Frenchman, Louis Jacques Mande Daguerre. After Niepce's death, Daguerre invented the first commercial photographic process in 1839 which he called the daguerreotype. Although the daguerreotype was similar in many ways to the heliograph, Daguerre used the mercury vapors on a sensitized, silver-coated, copper plate to obtain a faster, more light sensitive product. The daguerreotype produced a positive image directly from the camera, so the entire process had to be repeated to produce more than one image.

The daguerreotype was probably the first photographic image most people saw and the first time in history that a person could see a photographic image of him or herself. The daguerreotype was sharp and extremely detailed. It was also beautiful with its silver background and hand-colored surface. Many still consider it the most beautiful of the photographic processes.

During the same period that Daguerre was developing his process, an Englishman was also perfecting a photographic process. His name was William Henry Talbot, his process was called a Calotype (later to be renamed the Talbotype). His process differed in several important ways from the daguerreotype. He made a paper negative that was used to produce a positive paper print. This meant that many copies could be made from one negative. Later when the enlarger (or solar camera as it was first called) was invented, prints could be made bigger than the negative.

There were problems with the Calotype process since the negative was not made of glass or plastic but rather of paper. A very soft image was produced because of the paper fibers. Waxing the paper improved the sharpness but still did not produce the clarity of the daguerreotype. Later, the paper negative was oiled which again increased the quality of the image. The image produced from the negative was printed on a "salted print paper" which did not provide a sharp, contrasting image. The silver image was made up of specks of silver salted throughout the paper fibers. Finally Talbot, unlike Daguerre, patented his process and forced photographers to pay for the right to use his Calotype process.

In 1842, a print process called cyanotype was developed by Sir John Herschel, an English scientist and astronomer who also coined the words "photography", "negative" and "positive". The cyanotype is known today as the "blueprint". The process was not considered a major photographic process. It was mostly used in the reproduction fields and by children to produce photograms.

In 1848, the albumen process was invented by Abel Niepce de Saint-Victor. He was related to the inventor of photography, Nicephore Niepce. This process was a glass plate coated with albumen which acted as a binder for the silver nitrate layer. The albumen process produced a very fine negative image but was very slow when compared to other processes of the time. Because of its fine rendering of detail, it was mostly used as a positive slide material printed from a wet collodion plate to produce a lantern slide or for photographing landscapes. Prints made from these plates were initially salted paper prints.

In 1852, Frederick Scott Archer developed the wet collodion process or the "wet plate". This process produced a glass plate negative that could be printed onto paper and produce a positive image. The wet plate had to be coated by the photographer in the dark and exposed in the camera before it dried. Once it dried, it lost much of its light sensitivity. Photographers who worked in the field had to have a wagon complete with darkroom or a railroad car which was specially equipped. This process did not allow the photographer to just aim and shoot. Everything had to be set up prior to the coating of the emulsion.

Offshoots of the collodion process were the ambrotype (sometimes called melainotypes) and the tintype. Both used the collodion emulsion. An ambrotype was a collodion negative coated on glass. The color of the negative is the opposite of that seen in our modern films. It was not a black image but a light cream color. If the cream-colored glass negative was put in front of a black surface, it became a positive image. It did not have the brilliancy of a daguerreotype, but it was less expensive. Photographers soon started to replace daguerreotypes with ambrotypes and the middle classes could now afford photographs of themselves.

When wet collodion emulsion was coated onto a black metal (iron) it was called a tintype. The cream-colored negative against the black metal produced a positive image. The image was not very good when compared with a daguerreotype or an ambrotype, but it was cheaper and non-breakable. Since the tintype did not require a case, it was easy to mail. Neither the ambrotype or tintype could be made in any copies since the negative actually became the positive image.

The albumen print paper process, although invented in 1850, became prominent during and after the Civil War. This allowed a photographer to coat a piece of paper with the emulsion, let it dry and sandwich it with the negative in a printing frame. It was taken out into the light and left until the image looked right. The photographer then took it inside and stopped the process chemically. This process concept was called print out paper or "P.O.P.". Since, unlike the daguerreotype, ambrotype or the tintype, more than one positive print could be made from a single negative, mass production was now possible. Albumen prints were so successful that a majority of the history of the United States from the Civil War to the 1890s was recorded on albumen paper.

The first photographic print size used for trading and calling cards was the carte-de-visite and the cabinet card which followed. These cards became the standard for portrait print sizes. They were popular through the early 1900s.

After the Civil War, many photographers moved out West, recording new discoveries as the railroads pushed toward the Pacific Ocean. Photographs were used to persuade Congress to set aside land for parks and to convince people to come West to visit or settle. The final image was the same size as the image recorded in the camera. To make the image large enough for advertising purposes, large cameras were built that required several people to set up.

In the late 19th century, photography again changed drastically. Although enlargers, or solar cameras as they were initially called, had been invented in 1864, few were used because of the long time exposures required. However, in the 1890s when the faster bromide developing-out papers were available, enlargers were used to enlarge the image. Initially the sun was used as a source of light, but later oil, gas and electric arc light were used. Albumen paper was not light-sensitive enough for artificial light which eventually led to its disuse.

A process called the crayon print was produced during the early days of enlarging photographs. Often large prints were produced that were very soft focus and low contrast. The photographer would then use a black crayon or charcoal pencil to draw in the details, such as hair and facial characteristics. The effect was totally dependent on the artistic capabilities of the photographer.

The wet plate or collodion process was replaced with the dry plate or gelatin process in the 1880s. This allowed the photographer to go into the field with precoated glass plates ready for the camera. The quality and repeatability of the emulsions helped the photographer develop more precise controls on the process. At this point, photography as it is known today became a reality.

Glass plates gave way to film, allowing the cameras to greatly reduce in size. It was quite fashionable to be an amateur photographer. Cameras were now easy to use, small and lightweight. No longer was the photographic portrait just for the wealthy; now even the poorest individual was probably photographed sometime during his or her life.

Photography also became respected as an artform during the last of the 19th and beginning of the 20th centuries. In Britain there was the Linked Ring movement and in the United States the Photo-Secessionists. Master photographers such as Clarence White, Edward Steichen and Alfred Stieglitz developed the unique characteristics of the photographic image.

Prior to this period, photography was used primarily to record scenes or portraits. Now a photograph became interesting in its own right. A pioneering group of photographers, the f./64 Group, broke away from the soft out-of-focus look that mimicked paintings and concentrated on sharp focus images. The new direction was led by such photographers as Edward Weston, Ansel Adams, Edward Steichen, and Alfred Stieglitz. Much of their work was done on platinum or silver based emulsions. These are very stable and have endured.

Photography was started by scientists and has developed into a part of the human fabric, allowing people to see their family generations and to record their lives. As a record of the history of individual families, photography has played a major part in the lives of people.

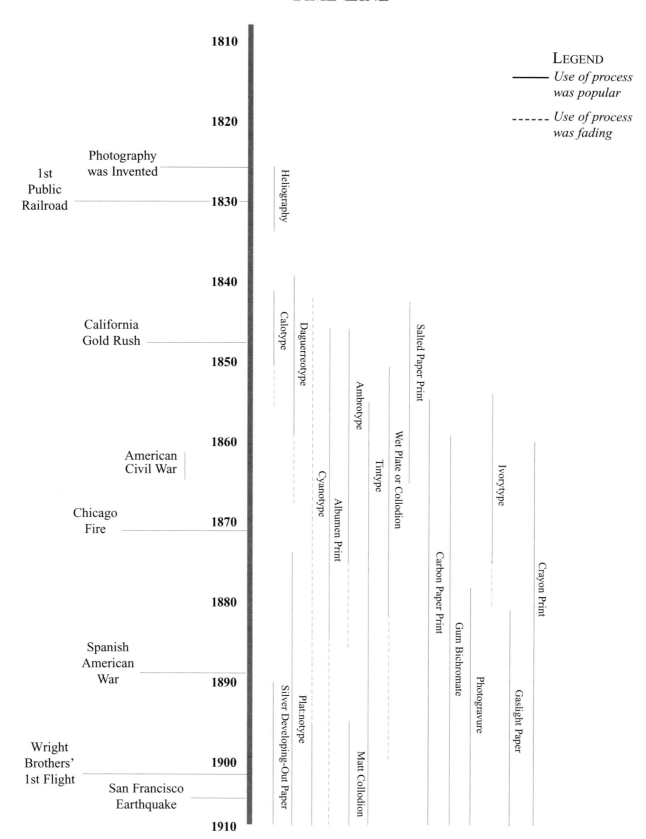

12 *Framing Photography*

Timeline

Historical Events (left side):
- Sinking of the Titanic — 1910
- World War I
- 1920
- Stock Market Crash — 1930
- Great Depression
- World War II — 1940
- 1950 — Korean War
- 1960 — Vietnam War
- America's First Moon Landing — 1970
- 1980
- Persian Gulf War — 1990
- 2000

Photographic Processes (right side):
- Oil Pigment
- Gaslight Paper
- Photogravure
- Gum Bichromate
- Matt Collodion POP
- Tintype
- Platinotype
- Cyanotype
- Silver Developing Out Paper
- Dye Transfer
- Kodacolor
- Ilfochrome Classic (Cibachrome)
- Polaroid
- Resin-coated materials
- Ultrastable
- EverColor
- Computer Generated Images

Framing Photography 13

Early Presentation Techniques/Methods

The photographer made a presentation of the photograph by putting it into a case, mounting it in an album, folder or on cardboard.

By identifying the presentation technique—the case or mount—the date and origin of an antique photograph will be easier to determine.

Cases

Moroccan Case
Moroccan leather, which was usually colored a maroon or black, covers a frame of fur pine wood sticks (rails). A thin wood sheet was attached to the back of the frame. The cover was also made of Moroccan leather with leather hinges, a brass clasp and a velvet or paper liner. The Moroccan case was initially used to protect the daguerreotype, but was then used for the ambrotype and tintype. It was employed for much of the British and European production and some American work. After 1854, much of the American photographers used the Union case.

Moroccan Case

American Union Case
This was a type of case used for daguerreotypes, ambrotypes, and tintypes. It was molded out of a thermoplastic made out of sawdust and varnish. It was introduced in the 1850s. During the early 20th century, these cases were used for carrying cigarettes; the photographs they held were probably discarded and lost. The Union case was very ornate compared to other cases such as the Moroccan case. Today, the case may be more valuable than the photograph inside.

American Union Case

Cards

Carte-de-Visite
The carte-de-visite was invented in France in 1854 and introduced into the United States in 1859. It started as an albumen print mounted onto a card, but was changed to other emulsions in the late 1800s. Cartes-de-visite were like baseball cards of today. They were collected and many were autographed. Prints of Civil War leaders, politicians, royalty and actors were popular with collectors. A carte0de0visite print was approximately 2-1/2x3-1/2" and was mounted on a 2-1/2x4" card. The size of the carte was standard throughout the world. Production ended in 1905.

Carte-de-visite

14 *Framing Photography*

Cabinet Card
Introduced to the United States in 1866, a cabinet card was 4x5-1/2" print mounted onto a 4-1/2x6-1/2" card. This was used in the late 19th century and may have an albumen emulsion or several other emulsions depending on the photographer. Production stopped in the 1920s.

Stereograph (Stereo Card)
Stereographs were introduced to the United States in 1851. Stereographs were two nearly identical images which, when viewed side-by-side, created the illusion of a three-dimensional images. The images were on paper, tissue, metal or glass. Originally, stereographs on paper were taken on the Calotype paper negative and printed onto salted paper print material.

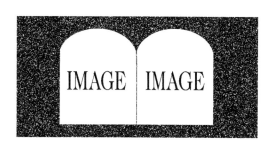

The stereo card is a piece of cardboard usually slightly bent from top to bottom. The cardboard is very acidic and will easily break if roughly handled. The card is usually about 3-1/2x7", containing two images about 3x3" rounded at the top.

Other Card Photographs
Actual sizes are shown on page 89.

Boudoir	5-1/4x8-1/2"	
Imperial	7-7/8x9-7/8", 6-7/8x9-7/8"	
Minette	1-1/2x2-3/8"	
Panel	4x8-1/4"	
Promenade	4-1/8x7-1/2", 4x7"	1850*
Victoria	3-1/4x5"	1870*

*the year it was introduced to the United States

From left to right: tintype, carte-de-visite, cabinet card.

Framing Photography 15

Photo Albums

Tintype, Carte-de-Visite & Cabinet Card
Early photographic albums were produced to protect collections of tintypes and cartes-de-visite. These albums have large mat pages and a clasp. They protected the photograph well because the clasp prevented environmental gases from damaging the photographic emulsions and the wide mat created a seal around the photograph.

Cardboard
A photography album made of black paper pages and black paper corner mounts. Black pages and black corner mounts are highly acidic. Extreme care should be taken with an early album since the paper is now weak and brittle. Use a thin spatula to remove a card photograph from an album page.

The photographs may come in direct contact with each other since they are stored face-to-face. Any moisture softens the gelatin emulsion and if two photographs are facing each other and touching, they will become permanently attached.

In addition to black corner mounts, the photographs may have been attached using rubber cement, tape or water-soluble pastes. It is recommended to remove these adhesives so that further damage does not occur.

Leather, Cloth & Paper Bound
Early photographic albums had large mat pages and a clasp. They kept the outside environmental gases away from the photographs.

Commercial Paper Folders
Decorated paper folders which are usually supplied by a photographic studio.

"Magnetic" Albums
The photographs are placed on a sticky page and covered with plastic. This album causes the photographs to deteriorate prematurely. Color photographs kept in a magnetic album last around 13-18 years, which is considerably shorter than their normal life expectancy. Removal is very difficult.

An English album from the 1860s.

Albums can provide protection from light, excessive handling and environmental pollution.

So called "magnetic albums", are pages with lines of adhesive to hold the photo and a sheet of plastic to cover the face of the photo. Unfortunately, over time the adhesive ages and holds the photo tightly to the backing as well as imparting a stain.

16 Framing Photography

Spray Coatings

Photographers use sprays on color photographs for two reasons: to provide ultraviolet protection and to hide imperfections caused by retouching or mounting. Picture framers may use sprays to conceal kinks, dirt, fingerprints, and excessive reflections on the emulsion of a photograph. Although a spray provides some benefits, it is not considered a conservation procedure. The spray can sometimes leave small, white specks on the emulsion or deposit areas of white residue if too much is applied.

If dirt gets onto or under a photograph while mounting and the print is an unsigned color print, the print may be sprayed with Sureguard-McDonald Pro-Tecta-Cote Matte® spray. The spray makes the bump on the surface almost disappear (the effect works especially well when the print is placed under regular glass), and also helps protect the print from ultraviolet light. Using this spray violates the conservation principle, and should only be used on unsigned chromogenic color prints that have no value and are simply to be displayed until they fade or are discarded. This should not be done to a print for which a negative is not available or one that is to be stored as part of a collection.

Sureguard-McDonald Pro-Tecta-Cote Matte spray eliminates glare on the surface of the print. Without this surface reflection the color appears to be more saturated.

There is some controversy about the use of a sealer on a chromogenic print causing possible starvation of oxygen in one of the three dye layers and other possible problems. However, from experience, when placing half of a print under the spray and the other half without, the print under the spray looks much better than the part without the spray. Fading is already easily recognizable on the side that has not been spray coated. Once again, this is not a conservation-approved technique but it seems to look great and extend the life of the print.

Most photographic conservators will not endorse spraying a photograph. There are many commercial labs that use spray lacquers on photographs to cover retouching. Just as with art on paper, conservation handling would be the best protection for a photograph using techniques that do not in any way change the photograph. Sprays cannot be completely cleaned off.

> *Seek approval from the owner of the photography before applying a spray.*

> *Using this spray violates the conservation principle, and should only be used on unsigned chromogenic color prints that have no value and are simply to be displayed until they fade or are discarded.*

Identification Chart

	Dates				Substrate													
	Dated from 1822-1865*	Dated from 1866-1929*	Dated from 1930-present*	Dated from 1990 to present	in a case	uncased	mounted on card**	mounted in card or paper folder	on uncoated paper	on coated paper	on translucent paper	on resin-coated paper	on polyester base	on smooth cut glass	on rough cut glass	on metal	appears to be on ivory	on film
Albumen Negative	X					X			X						X			
Albumen Print	X	X				X	X			X								
Ambrotype	X	X			X										X			
Calotype Negative	X					X			X		X							
Calotype Print (salt print)	X					X			X									
Carbon Print		X	X			X			X									
Chromogenic Paper			X			X				X		X						
Computer Generated Electronic Images				X						X	X***		X					X
Crayon Print		X				X	X		X									
Cyanotype	X	X				X			X									
Daguerrotype	X				X											X		
Dye Transfer		X				X				X								
EverColor			X			X				X			X					
Gaslight Paper		X	X			X				X								
Gum Bichromate		X	X			X					X							
Ilfochrome (Cibachrome)			X			X				X			X					
Ivorytype	X	X			X						X				X			
Kodachrome		X	X			X												X
Matt Collodion Print		X				X	X			X								
Oil Pigment Print		X				X			X		X	X						
Photogravure		X				X			X									
Platinotype		X	X			X			X									
Polaroid			X			X						X						
Salted Paper Print	X					X			X									
Silver Gelatin Print		X	X			X	X			X								
Tintype	X	X	X		X	X	X									X		
Ultrastable			X			X				X			X					
Wet Collodion Plate	X	X				X								X				

* Dates have been selected to reflect the highest production periods.
** Carte-de-visite, cabinet, etc., (see page 14-15)

*** Although the best detailed computer prints are printed on coated paper, any substrate that will accept ink can be used, even cloth such as canvas or cotton.

18 *Framing Photography*

	SURFACE					IMAGE CHARACTERISTICS															
has a matte surface	has a glossy surface	paper fibers show through under 30x	paper fibers show partially through under 30x	paper fibers do not show under 30x	soft focus	monochrome	color	has a blue image	changes from a positive to a negative with angle change	fading around edges or highlight areas/yellow cast	surface has a relief image on it	has mirroring dark or shadow areas	detail in deep shadows	attracted to a magnet	positive on black background	is a positive	is a negative	has mis-registration on edges	charcoal or pastel is visible	has uneven processing on edges	SEE PAGE	
	X					X				X							X					Albumen Negative
	X	X				X				X						X						Albumen Print
	X					X									X	X			X			Ambrotype
X		X		X	X												X					Calotype Negative
X		X		X	X											X						Calotype Print (salt print)
X		X	X	X		X					X					X	X					Carbon Print
X	X			X			X									X						Chromogenic Paper
X	X					X	X				X					X						Computer Generated Images
X			X	X	X													X				Crayon Print
X		X				X		X								X						Cyanotype
	X					X			X							X						Daguerrotype
X			X			X										X		X				Dye Transfer
			X			X										X						EverColor
X						X										X						Gaslight Paper
X		X		X	X											X						Gum Bichromate
X	X		X			X										X						Ilfochrome (Cibachrome)
			X	X												X						Ivorytype
								X								X						Kodachrome
X			X	X												X						Matt Collodion Print
X	X		X	X												X						Oil Pigment Print
X				X												X						Photogravure
X	X			X									X			X						Platinotype
			X		X	X										X	X					Polaroid
X	X			X												X						Salted Paper Print
X	X		X	X							X					X						Silver Gelatin Print
X				X										X	X	X			X			Tintype
X			X			X										X						Ultrastable
			X												X				X			Wet Collodion Plate

Framing Photography

Mat & Mount Boards

Mat and mount boards are divided into two main categories: those made of cotton and those made of wood pulp. Both of these categories are divided into several other categories based on their properties and processing.

Museum Board is a 100% cotton rag board. The board may be buffered (with calcium carbonate) or non-buffered. It is naturally free of lignin and acids. The coloring in these boards is minimal because the pigments used must be fade- and bleed-resistant, and totally free of contaminants.

There are two types of Conservation Board. One is made with a rag base and a cover sheet of alpha cellulose. The other is made entirely from alpha cellulose, which is a highly processed wood pulp. The lignin is removed, and buffering is added resulting in a buffered, acid-free board with an alkaline reserve. Some conservation boards are additionally treated with molecular traps designed to absorb pollutants. These may be useful as filler boards, but should not be placed in direct contact with valuable photos because of possible chemical reaction.

Standard Matboard, also called regular or paper matboard, is a wood pulp board containing lignin, although it is buffered with calcium carbonate. It is suitable for decorative framing but *not* for conservation framing. A higher quality white core version is also available, offering crisp white mat bevels, but this is also unsuitable for conservation framing.

Boards:

Archival PhotoRag Museum Board
This naturally acid- and lignin-free, non-buffered museum board is especially made for matting and mounting of certain photographs such as chromogenic, albumen, dye transfer, and other alkaline sensitive articles. It is 4-ply, 100% cotton, with solid color throughout, and a pH of 7.5(+/-.5).

Rag Mat
Rag Mat is a museum board made of 100% pure cotton fiber. It is naturally acid- and lignin-free. Crescent Classic Rag Mat 100 is a buffered, layered, extra rigid board. Rag Mat 100 is a solid, one layer board. Rag Mat may be used as a matting or a mounting board.

Acid-Free White Mounting Board
These are double-sided, white core, buffered, acid-free mounting boards. All components are treated with calcium carbonate to be pH neutral.

White Mounting Boards
These boards have a solid core news middle with a double-sided, smooth, buffered, acid-free, white surface. They are used for routine mounting. They are a good substrate for pressure-sensitive film, wet, spray and dry mounting.

Recycled Mounting Board
Recycled mounting boards are made using 100% recycled fiber buffered with calcium carbonate to be pH neutral. White both sides with recycled symbol imprint on one side. Available in single and double thickness.

Regular Matboard
Regular matboard, also called paper mat, has a buffered acid-free pulp core and backing paper. It is available in a extensive color range with many different surface textures and finishes.

All Black Mounting Board
Solid black throughout and both sides are usable. Used for mounting photographs and other artwork, and as a presentation board.

Competition Mounting Board
A triple-thick (.120) board designed especially for photography competitions. Meets Professional Photographers of America exhibition mounting requirement for thickness. Available in two colors: solid black or double-sided, buffered, acid-free white surface papers.

Regular, Acid-Free, and Rag Foam Center Board
Foam center board is a lightweight, inert, white, plastic center faced on both sides with white clay-coated paper. Available in several thicknesses. Acid-free foam center board is faced on both sides with acid-free barrier papers, and the Rag version is faced with rag paper. Foam center board can be used with all mounting methods; however when heat mounting, the heat should not exceed 180° F.

Supersmooth®
A bright white, ultra-smooth surface on a rigid core. Constructed from multiple layers of very dense, compressed white refined wood fibers. Both surface and core are non-yellowing and acid-free. Excellent for mounting high-gloss photos and glossy artwork, or whenever smoothness is important. Available in several sizes either plain or pre-coated with Perfect Mount™ adhesive. Also available in Competition Board.

Chapter 2
Types of Photographic Processes
In Alphabetical Order
Albumen

Years in Use: 1847–1906

Overview: The paper support was coated with egg white, filling the small pores of the paper to create a smooth surface. This was followed by a silver emulsion coating. This print process was very successful and was used for many years as a contact paper. Most of the Civil War photographic documentation was printed on albumen paper. The albumen layer was very thin and only coated on one side.

Identifying Characteristics:
- Signs of fading include yellowing of highlights.
- The overall color can be red, brown, purple, or yellow.
- Paper fibers will show through the albumen binder and will be visible in all areas of the image if viewed through a 30x magnifier.
- If the albumen was double coated as it was in later years, the fibers are often harder to see.
- There is no relief image. The surface was made shiny by burnishing.
- Possible fading around edges.

Care & Handling: Albumen prints are unstable and may not survive much longer if not properly stored. A yellowing of the highlight areas is caused by silver becoming silver sulfide. No known technique has been developed to counteract the reaction.

The picture on the left has been handled and exposed to light and contaminants. The picture on the right has been stored in an album without exposure to light and contaminants.

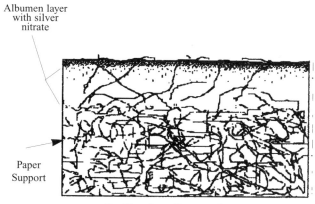

Profile of an albumen photograph.

Do not immerse albumen in water; cracks in the surface of albumen can widen during the drying stage. Since albumen is a protein, it will shrink and crack. It is very sensitive to changes in temperature and relative humidity. As it softens it swells, and as it dries it shrinks and cracks. Mold will grow in over 70% relative humidity.

Possible Presentation Techniques:
If the albumen print is mounted, it may be mounted on:
- Carte-de-visite
- Cabinet card
- Stereograph
- Boudoir card
- Imperial card
- Minette card
- Panel card
- Promenade card
- Victoria card

(actual card sizes are on page 89)

Some photographers using this process:
- Matthew Brady
- Julia Margaret Cameron
- Frances Frith
- Eadweard Muybridge

Mounting Recommendations:
Albumen prints are unstable and may not survive much longer if not properly stored. They may only survive another 60 years.
Board: non-buffered cotton rag
Process: sink mat or float mount

Framing Recommendations:
Frame: hinged, double mat
Cover mats: double mat for unmounted prints
Glazing: UV

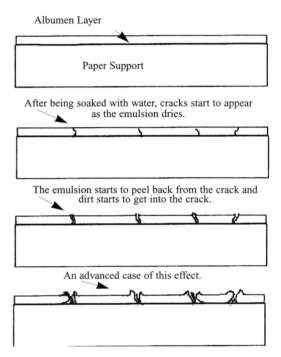

Deterioration of an albumen print

22 *Framing Photography*

AMBROTYPE

Years in Use: 1847–1880

Overview: Invented in 1852 by Frederick Scott Archer. It was a variation of the wet collodion process or wet plate process. Silver nitrate was dissolved in collodion and hand-coated onto glass and while still wet, exposed and processed. After processing, the resulting negative image was a light cream color and, when backed with black material, it became a positive image.

The black backing was created several ways:
       a) paint was applied to the back of the glass plate
       b) fabric was used behind the plate
       c) paint applied to the case
       d) with a dark red, amber color glass.
Since it was considerably cheaper than the daguerreotype, it had replaced the daguerreotype by the Civil War.

Identifying Characteristics:
- Glass negative
- Will not attract a magnet
- Will not change from a negative to a positive as it is moved
- Often hand-tinted
- Black backing such as paper, paint or velvet
- Some were done on deep red glass

The ambrotype is a cream-colored emulsion coated on a glass plate. To produce a positive image, it must be placed on a black or dark surface.

The top photograph is an ambrotype against black and in its case. The photograph below is against a white card so that the negative image is apparent.

Care & Handling: An ambrotype can be cleaned by an expert. Improper cleaning will cause loss of emulsion or scratching. Collodion dissolves in alcohol.

- Deteriorated cover glass.
    Handling: Remove and replace cover glass.

- Actual flaking collodion binder layers.
    Handling: Take ambrotype to photo conservator for any possible solution. Flaking will only get worse without the right technique.

- Broken primary support.
    Handling: See a photographic conservator. In most cases a copy will have to be made to save the image.

- Deteriorated backing.
    Handling: Remove ambrotype carefully from case or frame and replace or repair the backing. Most backings can be replaced with a photographic sheet of black and white film that has been light fogged and archivally processed, or a piece of smooth black rag matboard. The ambrotype emulsion should be on the opposite side of the support glass away from the replacement black material. If there is enamel paint on the ambrotype do not remove it. Just add the new black backing.

Possible Presentation Techniques:
  • Union case
  • Moroccan leather case
  • Frame with a hanging chain

Mounting Recommendations:
    Board: Use unbuffered cotton rag if the ambrotype is in leather case
    Buffered or unbuffered cotton rag if it is loose
    Process: Use an object box or display case for a cased photograph and a sink mat or float mat for an uncased photograph.

Framing Recommendations:
    Cover Mats: Double mat for uncased prints
    Glazing: UV

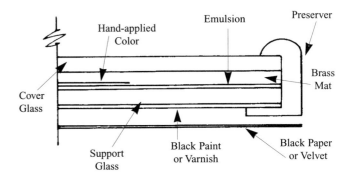

Profile of ambrotype package.

CALOTYPE (TALBOTYPE)

Years in Use: 1841–1856

Overview: This was the first negative/positive process. The process used a paper negative which resulted in a soft grainy appearance. The silver grains were salted throughout the paper fibers. This paper negative was then improved by waxing it so that the fibers were less noticeable. This improved the quality of the image but it still did not compare with the daguerreotype. The negative was contact printed onto a salted paper (until Albumen prints came into use) and produced very soft high-contrast prints. The Calotype lost popularity after the wet collodion process was discovered.

The Calotype was invented by William Henry Talbot in 1841.

Identifying Characteristics:
- Under a 30x microscope, the paper fibers can be seen pushing through the image.
- The paper negative was often waxed for translucency (beeswax).
- The skies were often retouched on the paper negative. India ink was used to paint out the clouds.
- The image had little detail.

Care & Handling: Since this is an old process, great care should be taken while handling. Do not attempt any work on it. Do the framing with guidance from a photographic conservator. Because of the historic value of the piece, it may be suggested to the owner that it should be offered to a museum for proper care and storage. A copy of the image can be made, so that the family will still have the original image. This process should be handled by a photographic conservator who is an expert old emulsions.

Mounting Recommendations:
    Board: non-buffered cotton rag
    Process: If the photograph is mounted, use a sink mat or float mount. If unmounted, use hinges.

Framing Recommendations:
    Frame: hinged, double frame
    Cover Mats: double mat with spacers between mats
    Glazing: UV

Possible Presentation Techniques:
- Mounted on a card
- Tipped into a page
- Loose

Some Photographers Using This Process:
- David Octavius Hill
- Robert Hill
- John Whistler
- Robert Adamson
- Hippolyte Bayard

CARBON PRINT PROCESS

Years in Use: 1855–Present

Overview: The carbon print process was invented by Alphonse Poitevin in 1855. The carbon print will not fade easily. It is often mistaken for a woodburytype which is a photomechanical process and not a photograph. A carbon print can be any size.

Identifying Characteristics:
- Will have an image relief on the print surface.
- It may show pigment specks under 30x magnification.
- Although almost any color could be used, the standard colors were brown and purple.
- There may be large cracks in the dark shadow areas.
- Little or no fading.

Care & Handling: It is made of a heavy coat of animal protein gelatin and should be handled as a fine piece of art on paper.

Possible Presentation Techniques:
- Mounted
- Loose

Some Photographers Using This Process:
- Adolph Braun
- William Huston
- W.J. Kuhns

Mounting Recommendations:
  Board: Non-buffered cotton rag
  Process: If the photograph is mounted, use a sink mat or float mount. If it is unmounted, use hinges.

Framing Recommendations:
  Cover Mats: double mat with spacers between mats
  Glazing: UV

The carbon print process was invented by Alphonse Poitevin in 1855.

CHROMOGENIC PRINTS
(KODACOLOR®, EKTACOLOR®, KONICA®, AGFA®, FUJICOLOR®)

Years in Use: 1942– Present

Overview: The color print was first introduced as Kodacolor with the other processes, such as Ektacolor, following shortly after. Other brands include Konica color, Agfa color and Fujicolor. Most of the chromogenic print papers will begin to show color shift between 15 to 20 years.

Identifying Characteristics:
- Early color prints often have the date of the image printed on the back.
- Prints taken after 1968 that are on resin-coated (RC paper) should have the name of the paper manufacturing company on the back.
- No fibers show through surface when seen under 30x magnification.
- Studio name may be stamped or printed on the front surface
- If over 20 years old, may show advanced fading.
- Prints from the 1950s will show considerable, dark fading. There will be noticeable orange color where there should be white.

Care & Handling: Use white gloves when handling this type of photograph. Care should be taken to insure that the paper does not kink. The process is very unstable and can withstand only limited display time before showing fading. Serious collectors will often store their color collection in humidity sealed containers in a refrigerator to reduce chemical fading, often called dark fading. Photographs displayed in fluorescent lighting or direct sunlight will begin fading in less than 10 years. Care should always be taken to inform the customer of the fragility of the image.

Possible Presentation Techniques:
- Mounted
- Unmounted

Mounting Recommendations:
　Board: Non-buffered cotton rag
　Process: Use hinges for signed, limited editions or older images. Unsigned prints can be mounted using the following methods: dry, wet, spray or pressure-sensitive.

Framing Recommendations:
　Cover mats: Double mat
　Glazing: UV

Framing Photography 27

Computer Generated Electronic Images

The use of the computer for copying and restoring photographs has become an important method for photo reproduction, soon perhaps the primary one. Beginning in the early 1990s this rapidly began to replace older techniques. Photographs can easily be scanned into a computer. The images can then be altered in many ways. Incomplete images can be made whole. Missing parts replaced. Dust and scratches can be eliminated. Black and white images can be made in color, and vice versa. Images can be enlarged or reduced in size. Images can be sent to other computers via the Internet.

Usually at some point in time the image will be made into a paper print or a film negative. The negative will probably be 35mm. The negative is used to produce a normal photographic print.

If the computer image is made into a paper print instead of a negative, we enter a new and confusing world of image products. The typical consumer assumes that these images are the same as any other photograph. In fact they are quite different, and have a much shorter life expectancy. Framers should be careful. These images are still very temporary in nature and many are very easily damaged by heat, moisture and finger prints.

Ink Jet or Laser Prints

These are often produced on home and office printers. At a typical 720 dots per inch resolution, color ink dots can be seen by close inspection. A continuous tone would be possible in resolutions above 1800dpi. With very sophisticated ink jet printers like an Iris printer, the dots are blurred, causing them to blend. Very smooth or glossy coated papers produce the best jet or laser photo prints. Ink jet and laser printers are not usually considered adequate for a professional photographic print.

The life expectancy of the print is based on the dyes used in printing. Few are good enough to compare with the typical chromogenic photograph. Most will fade in less than six years. The use of heat in mounting is not recommended unless a test is made first, since some of these printers use heat to dispense the ink. In the future, expect nearly archival black or gray inks to be introduced. Color is another story; as long as dye is involved the life cannot be very long. However, there are currently efforts to produce oil emulsified inks that may last up to 30 years.

We now enter the new and confusing world of image products. The typical consumer assumes these images are the same as any other photograph. In fact they are quite different, and have a much shorter life expectancy.

The ink jet printer places dots of ink in random patterns much like the simulation shown here. The number of dots varies from about 180dpi to as high as 1400 in common business or PC printers. On special paper it is difficult to see the dots at above 720dpi, but the dots can be seen under magnification. If in color, the color dots are overprinted with other colors causing some smoothing of the image.

DYE SUBLIMATION PRINTS

Many photo shops produce the final copy of a computer-generated print using a computer printer. This is often a Dye Sublimation printer, which produces a print that must be laminated to protect it from the environment. Non-laminated prints will often turn a red color and start to deteriorate soon after production. Some photo shops copy this "work print" onto a normal color or black and white film, then print the photo on normal photo paper. The longer life prints are those printed in black and white on fiber based paper.

To the naked eye, dye sublimation prints appear to be normal, continuous tone photographs. Under magnification patterns or lines can be seen. These lines are parallel to the printer head movement. The lines are made by a heated printer head passing over a plastic sheet of heat-sensitive ink. The ink softens and is transferred with pressure to a paper support. The support is often thin paper with a smooth surface. Since these prints are made with heat, any heat applied later may cause damage.

An image relief is sometimes another identifying sign. Since each color is applied with a different pass of the printer or at a different time, the different layers can sometimes be seen if you look at the image from the edge of the print.

The dye sublimation print is often identified by a series of parallel lines of ink. These lines can be seen with a 30 to 100x magnification loupe. The lines are variable in width, which produces the image. The vertical version shown here is called "portrait" format. The horizontal version is called "landscape" format.

The photograph on the left is a black and white print on a fiber based paper from 1940. The copy on the right is a dye sublimation print made on a do-it-yourself machine at a local photo shop.

To the naked eye, and even under 10X magnification, the two look almost identical; but at 30X magnification, the lines that make up the new copy become visible. Comparing one next to the other, the dye sublimation print has a pinkish tone and the contrast is lessened; also, the paper is very thin and smooth.

The original photo has great longevity. The copy will probably begin to change color and deteriorate within a few years.

Original Monochrome (Black & White) 1940   *Dye Sublimation Print 1999*

Framing Photography 29

CRAYON PRINT

Years in Use: 1860s –1900s

Overview: A print on which a photographer drew in the detail with charcoal or pastels.

It was popular after the invention of the solar camera or early enlarger. The solar camera was developed before light-sensitive enlarging paper so it was difficult to produce an enlarged print with the contact paper being too slow. Therefore, to achieve a better enlarged image at a faster rate, a low density image was made with only some of the detail showing. Since the image was enlarged beyond the capacity of the optics of the time, the image was very soft and out-of-focus. There were no sharp lines such as hair and eyelashes; these were added by the photographer.

Photographers would also underexpose a print to insure that a background was not shown except as a white sheet. Details would also be painted on these prints.

Identifying Characteristic:
- The actual image is soft focus.
- The charcoal drawing is visible.

Care & Handling: Remove the wood back of its original framing and replace with rag matboard. Do not touch the surface with fingers because the pastels may rub off.

Possible Presentation Techniques:
- Loose
- Framed without a mat

Framing Recommendations:
   Cover Mats: Non-buffered cotton rag
   Backing Board: Non-buffered rag
   Glazing: UV

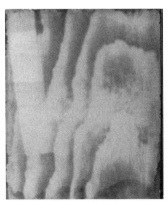

The reverse side of the crayon print mountboard is stained with the imprint of the acidic wood backing (right). A ghost of the work order is seen on the paper board backing. It afforded a bit of protection from the acidic wood backing board.

The original wood backing.

Cyanotype (Blueprint Process)

Years in Use: 1842– Present
                Most popular from 1895 to 1920

Overview: The cyanotype was invented by Sir John Herschel in 1842. Sir Herschel, better known in the field of astronomy, also coined the terms "photography", "positive" and "negative". The cyanotype is still used today for architectural or mechanical drawings.

Final Image Material is made of iron compounds. The cyanotype was also used as a means of producing photograms for school children in the early 20th century.

Identifying Characteristics:
- A white image with blue shadows or a blue image on white.
- Prints are primarily blue but they can be toned gray, red, brown, black, green or violet.
- The support is paper.
- There is not a binder.
- Paper fibers will show under 30x magnification

Care & Handling: The cyanotype is light-sensitive and should not be placed on permanent display. Copies should be made and the original should be stored in the dark. It has been shown that if fading has taken place, it is possible to rejuvenate the image if it is placed in the dark.

Possible Presentation Techniques:
- Mounted on a cardboard backing
- Loose

Mounting Recommendations:
    Board: Non-buffered cotton rag
    Process: If the photograph is mounted, use a sink or float mat. If it is unmounted, use hinges.

Framing Recommendations:
    Frame: Hinged frame with a copy of the cyanotype on the outside and the original on the inner frame. When closed, the cyanotype is in the dark. This frame is described on page 74.
    Cover Mats: Double mat with spacers between for unmounted photograph.
    Glazing: UV

Profile of cyanotype emulsion.
The cyanotype is a salted paper that used iron salts instead of silver. There was no surface binder or baryta layers and the salts were in the paper fibers much like silver salted papers. The surface appeared to be matt since the paper fibers were not coated.

Framing Photography 31

DAGUERREOTYPE

Years in Use: 1839–1870

Overview: The daguerreotype was invented by Louis Jacques Mande Daguerre in 1839. It is a direct positive process which means there is no negative for duplication. Indoor portraits were most common. Outdoor photographs were taken, but they are very rare. Exposure time was long and required subjects to hold still for long periods (10 to 15 minutes before 1841 and 2-3 minutes there after).

Identifying Characteristics:
- A thin, copper sheet plated with silver.
- Sealed under glass.
- The standard plate size was 6-1/2x8-1/2" but the most popular sizes were the quarter plate (3-1/4x4-1/4") and the sixth plate (3-1/4"x3-3/4").
- By moving or rocking the plate, a negative or positive image can be seen.
- The silver surface reflects like a mirror.
- Image is delicate and brilliant.
- Color was often applied by hand. Small dots of paint were used on buttons and jewelry.
- Larger areas were colored with sifted pigment sprinkled through a stencil or applied with a very fine brush.
- Not attracted to a magnet.

Care & Handling: Never attempt to clean the surface of the silver plate since it scratches easily. Just brushing the surface of the image can break the silver lumps off. Do not take the daguerreotype out of the case. Any breaking of the sealed case or inner package will expose the silver image to modern air pollutants and the plate will tarnish with sulfur contamination. Unless an image is in danger of being lost, do not clean the silver plate because of the probable loss of either the image or the hand-applied color.

The common causes of damage:
- Silver sulfide tarnishing
    Handling: can be removed by an expert, but may return.
- Mold growth
    Handling: can not be removed, store in cool dry environment to retard further damage.
- Evenly distributed black spots
    Handling: cannot be removed; store in dry cool environment to retard further damage.
- Green crystals
    Handling: can be removed but may return.

Possible Presentation Techniques:
- Union case
- Moroccan leather case
- Small frame with a hanging chain

Mounting Recommendations:
  Board: Non-buffered cotton rag
  Process: Sink mount or float mount

Framing Recommendations:
The framer should always frame both the case and plate; do not separate. Often the case is more valuable than the daguerreotype. If the case is to be framed, it should be done in such a way that the viewer can see the design of the outside surface of the case (a mirror or a glass back). See page 70 for description of frame.

Glazing: UV

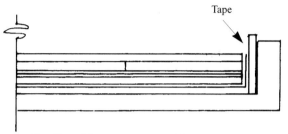

Profile of daguerreotype without a preserver.
This profile does not have a preserver. The tape is cut at the top of the glass cover so that it does not show. The tape usually completely covers the bottom of the package.

Hand-Tinted Daguerreotype
Many daguerreotypes had color pigment added by an artist, often a portrait painter. The color pigment was added with a fine brush or sifted on the image and set by blowing warm, moist air from the mouth. Almost all later daguerreotypes were colored. This process was also popular on ambrotypes and tintypes.

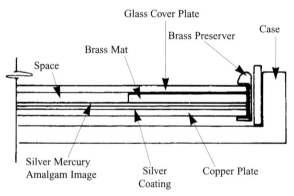

Profile of daguerreotype with a preserver
The imagery package is held together with a tape or animal membrane and a metal preserver. The preserver is fitted around the taped glass and metal package and bent around the back. The brass mat prevents the glass cover plate from touching the silver image.

Dye Transfer

Years in Use: 1946 – Present

Overview: This process can be used to produce either color transparencies or negatives, although transparencies are the most popular. Separation negatives were used to break down the color image into three color negatives. These negatives are exposed on special matrix film that has a gelatin emulsion. Once processed, the gelatin emulsion image is in relief. It is then soaked in the appropriate color dye and rolled onto a paper support. The dye is transferred and the next matrix is applied. The process is complicated and requires a lot of time to complete. The three images have to be exactly registered so that a double or triple image does not result.

Identifying Characteristics:
- The edge of the image will show three color images superimposed on each other.
- Paper will be fiber-based.
- Ink layers may be visible at edges.

Care & Handling: The dye transfer is likely to last at least 40 years under incandescent lighting; less if exposed to direct daylight.

Possible Presentation Techniques:
- Mounted (edges may have been trimmed off)
- Loose

Mounting Recommendations:
  Board: Non-buffered cotton rag
  Process: If the photograph is mounted, use hinges, corner or edge mounts, sink mat.

Framing Recommendations:
  Cover Mats: Double mat with spacer between mats for a unmounted photograph
  Glazing: UV

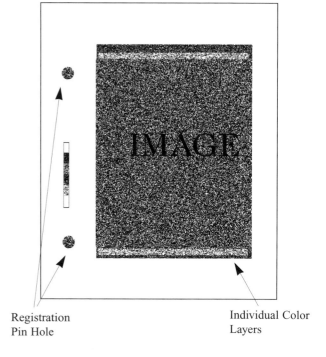

Registration Pin Hole

Individual Color Layers

The dye transfer print can be identified by seeing mis-registration between the different color layers. This is usually found opposite the side with the registration pin holes.

Each matrix sheet that is used to transfer a single color onto the print paper shrinks differently as it dries after processing.

Most of the final prints have had the color scales and holes cut off before being distributed. However, the mis-registration is often apparent, especially on larger prints.

EverColor™

Years in Use: 1991 – Present

Overview: The EverColor process begins with a high resolution digital scan of a negative, reflective artwork or transparency. The image is then electronically manipulated and output on color separation film. CMYK (Cyan, Magenta, Yellow and Black) colors are bonded one layer at a time to a polyester substrate.

The colors are placed on top of the substrate instead of being developed in the emulsion. The result is a hand-pulled print that is guaranteed not to fade or discolor under typical home, museum or gallery lighting for at least 200 years.

Identifying Characteristics:
- The name EverColor will be on the back.

Care & Handling:
- Handle as fine art on paper.

Possible Presentation Techniques:
- loose

Mounting Recommendations:
    Board: Buffered or non-buffered cotton rag
    Process: Use hinges since the photograph will most likely outlive the framing package.

Framing Recommendations:
    Cover Mats: Buffered or non-buffered cotton rag
    Glazing: UV or regular

This is a fine art print that begins with a high resolution digital scan.

GASLIGHT PAPER

Years in Use: 1881–1960

Overview: Gaslight paper was a contact printing paper that was too slow to be sensitive to gaslight so it could be handled safely in a room with gaslight. The photographer would load the paper into a contact frame and take it outside for the actual exposure. Gaslight paper was a gelatin, silver chloride emulsion coated on paper. The first emulsion was invented in 1881. A common name for this type of paper in the US was Velox® which was introduced in 1893. Gaslight paper was used primarily as a contact paper.

Identifying Characteristics:
- Usually a glossy surface paper, although matte versions were produced.
- Under 30x magnification, paper fibers rarely show in the highlight areas.
- A three layer emulsion: binder, baryta layer and the support.
- Gelatin emulsion will swell if a water drop is placed on it.

Care & Handling: Since the paper could be over a hundred years old, extreme care should be taken in handling this print material.

Possible Presentation Techniques:
- Mounted to cardboard
- Loose

Mounting Recommendations:
Board: Non-buffered cotton rag
Process: If the photograph is mounted, use a sink mat or float mount. If it is unmounted, use hinges, corner or edge mounts. Dry mounting may be used but it is recommended to obtain a waiver from the customer.

Framing Recommendations:
Cover Mats: Double mat for unmounted print
Glazing: UV

Profile of a gaslight paper print.

Gelatin emulsion will swell if a water drop is placed on it.

Gum or Bichromate Prints (Gum Dichromate)

Years in Use: 1858–1920s, although recent interest in this process has resulted in the production of kits for modern printing.

Overview: John Pouncy first exhibited gum prints in London in 1858. The imagery could be easily manipulated manually which allowed photographers to simulate chalk, pastels or paintings with the process. The process remained popular until the 1920s, although gum prints are still used for special effects by artists.

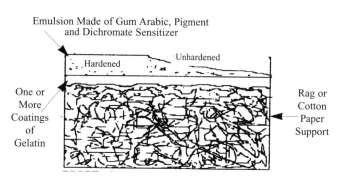

Profile of gum or bichromate print

Identifying Characteristics:
- The gum emulsion was usually coated on a matte or rough-surfaced paper.
- The image was slightly soft or hazy. Many times the imagery looked like it was brushed on.
- Colors could vary from black through the entire spectrum, although natural color was rarely attempted. Light red was often seen.
- The edge of the print may show brush strokes.

Care & Handling: The gum bichromate print was usually an art print and is valuable as an example of the period when photographers were attempting to elevate photography to an art. Care should be taken in handling this type of print. Inspect for any signatures or initials. Very few examples exist outside of museums. If unsure of the identification, contact a photo conservator.

Possible Presentation Techniques:
- Mounted to cardboard backing
- Loose

Some Photographers Using This Process:
- Robert Demachy
- Edward Steichen
- Clarence White
- Frank Eugene
- Alvin Langdon Coburn

Mounting Recommendations:
Board: Non-buffered cotton rag if the mat touches the emulsion; buffered if the mat does not touch the emulsion.
Process: Use hinges. Dry mounting or contact adhesives should never be used since this is a hand-coated product.

Framing Recommendations:
Since most of the finished gum prints are mounted on board, there is uncertainty about the quality of the board. Inspect the print and board carefully and check for acid burn from lignin breakdown. If there are no signs of acid burns, then mat and frame with buffered, lignin-free materials. If burn signs or mildew are present, make a copy and suggest to the customer that it be retired to a cool, dry storage location.

Under no conditions should it be placed on continuous display in a household or office environment. A conservator can remove the board if necessary. A photographic copy should be made of the print and the copy can be displayed.

Cover Mats: buffered or non-buffered cotton rag (if unmounted)
Glazing: UV glass or UV acrylic

ILFOCHROME CLASSIC® (CIBACHROME)

Years in Use: As Cibachrome from 1963 to 1991;
as Ilfochrome Classic from 1991 to Present

Overview: Ilfochrome Classic, the new name for Cibachrome, can last between twenty and forty years without fading, depending on the type. It is produced from a transparency and not a negative. There are two surfaces available in the Cibachrome process: a semi-matte surface on a paper substrate and an ultra-glossy surface on a polyester base.

Identifying Characteristics:
- High contrast
- Saturated colors
- Made from slides or positive transparencies

Care & Handling: The glossy version is so glossy that any fingerprints or kinks will show. Wear white cotton gloves. Do not touch the surface. Never brush a hand across or roll it up without a release paper cover. Dust particles will scratch the surface. Clean the surface with compressed air. Do not blow air from the mouth because a moisture droplet will mark the surface. Make sure that the surface of the photograph never touches the glazing.

Possible Presentation Techniques:
- Mounted
- Loose (unless produced for advertising.)

Mounting Recommendations:
Any permanent mounting technique will produce an orange peel effect. An orange peel effect is an uneven surface distortion created by the contouring of the photo emulsion to the substrate Pressure-sensitive adhesives will also cause an orange peel effect. Water-soluble adhesives, such as wheat paste, will not hold the plastic base.
    Board: Non-buffered cotton rag
    Process: Unlimited, unsigned prints may be dry mounted using the lowest temperature possible. For limited editions, use hinges. Spacers or mats must be used so that the surface of the photograph does not touch the glazing.
Framing Recommendations:
    Cover Mats: Double mat with spacers between mats for unmounted prints
    Glazing: UV

Never brush a hand across or roll it up without a release paper cover. Dust particles will scratch the surface.

IVORYTYPE

Years in Use: 1855–1876

Overview: The ivorytype was patented in 1855 by John J.E. Mayall. One version was a photograph printed on an emulsion coated on artificial ivory plates. The emulsion was either albumen or collodion.

A later version used two paper prints, one a transparent print paper and the other a normal opaque print stock. The transparent print was mounted on a glass plate and colored on the back. The second print was colored in the normal manner then mounted and sealed to the first print.

Identifying Characteristics:
- Hand-applied pigments were added after the ivory type was processed.
- The transparent print of a later version was mounted on a glass plate and colored on the back.
- Second print sealed to a transparent print.
- Substrate is artificial ivory.

Care & Handling: Care should be taken in any attempt to clean the ivorytype. Consultation with photograph conservator is a must. The ivorytype is fairly rare. Danger in delamination of the prints from the glass and breakdown of the color agent is possible.

Possible Presentation Techniques:
- Case
- Jewelry

Mounting Recommendations:
 Board: Non-buffered cotton rag if it is unmounted
 Process: If the ivorytype is unmounted, use a sink mat. If it is mounted, use an object box.

Framing Recommendations:
If the ivorytype is still intact in a case or frame, it should not be opened without consultation with a photography conservator. The Ivorytype should be copied with black and white film. A copy print that has been toned and oil-colored can be framed for continual viewing. If the actual Ivorytype is framed, it should be placed in an object box with an opaque door or curtain that is only opened when it is viewed. (See Project 10 as an example.)
 Moulding: Shadowbox
 Cover Mats: Non-buffered if it is unmounted or buffered if it is mounted.
 Glazing: UV

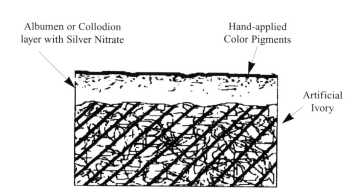

Profile of Ivorytype.

Although called an Ivorytype, the image was not made on ivory.

Framing Photography 39

Matt Collodion Printing-Out Paper (POP)

Years in Use: 1894–1930

Overview: The matt collodion process has proven very stable and was very popular. The use of both platinum and gold toners insured image stability.

Identifying Characteristics:
The matt collodion had the surface and color many gelatin print manufactures tried to copy which may make it difficult to identify the emulsion.
- The color hue of the print emulsion is near neutral with the shadows close to black.
- Has a matte surface.
- The staining action of platinum resulting in a transfer image on another print stored with it.
- A three-layer material which contains the base or paper substrate, the baryta layer and the collodion binder layer.
- Under a 30x magnification, paper fibers may be seen, especially in the highlight areas where the silver image is least dense.
- Appears to be very stable with no mirroring or fading.

Care & Handling: Since the image material is very stable only the mount is of concern. The matt collodion could be over 100 years old so take care during the movement and storage of the card. The card stock may be quite brittle from the breakdown of the lignin. Care should be taken to protect the surface from scratching and rubbing.

Possible Presentation Techniques:
- Carte-de-visite
- Cabinet card
- Stereograph
- Cabinet card
- Boudoir card
- Imperial card
- Minette card
- Panel card
- Promenade card
- Victoria card

(actual card sizes are on page 89)

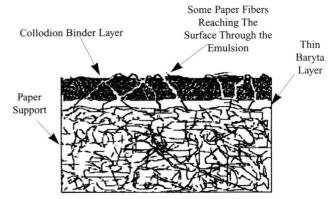

Profile of Matt Collodion Print.

Mounting Recommendations:
  Board: Buffered or non-buffered cotton rag
  Process: If the photograph is mounted, use a sink mat. If it is unmounted, use hinges.

Framing Recommendations:
  Cover Mats: double mat
  Glazing: UV

OIL PIGMENT

Years in Use: 1904-1930s

Overview: This process uses oil-based inks. Gelatin will harden in the areas that have been exposed to light. When the gelatin is soaked in water, it swells in the areas which are not exposed to light; allowing the water to get into the layer. Areas that have been exposed to light harden and water does not penetrate into the gelatin. Therefore, the oil based ink will not stick where the water is present; it will only stick to the print. A negative is used to produce the exposure, so the dark areas of the print will get the most light and therefore will retain the least amount of water, and the ink will stick there best.

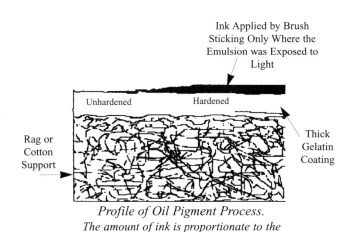

Profile of Oil Pigment Process.
The amount of ink is proportionate to the hardening of the gelatin.

Identifying Characteristics:
- Little detail in highlight areas.
- Matte surface.
- Used coating of gelatin to hold the ink.

Care & Handling: The image is a very stable process, but since the process is almost 100 years old, some paper substrates are beginning to harden. If it is mounted, then the mounting board is extremely acidic and very brittle. Handle with care.

Possible Presentation Techniques:
- Mounted (wet or dry mounting possible)
- Loose
- Tipped in

Photographer Using This Process:
- Robert Demachy

Mounting Recommendations:
   Board: Non-buffered cotton rag if mat is touching emulsion
   Process: Hinges or dry mounting

Photogravure

Years in Use: 1880s–1920s

Overview: The photogravure is a photochemical process that has extremely good definition. Many photographers had photogravure prints made directly off the negative without making a photographic print. This means that the photogravure print was the original; another version of the photogravure was the gravure screen.

Identifying Characteristics:
- An aquatint (grain) speckle and a plate mark.
- Flat
- Fine detail was possible.
- Any kind of paper stock matte or glossy could be used.
- Usually mounted on a separate page and often with a cover sheet.

Gravure Screen:
- An aquatint grain but no plate mark.
- Contained on a cylinder.
- Image was a cross-hatched, speckle aquatint.

Care & Handling: Although the image should be in excellent shape, the paper substrate may have physical damage such as foxing, acid burns and stains. Since the support may be quite brittle, care must be taken to prevent bending or kinking of the print. Provide good support when mounting.

Possible Presentation Techniques:
- Mounted (early examples may be wet mounted, later examples dry mounted)
- Loose
- Tipped in

Some Photographers Using This Process:
- Alfred Stieglitz
- Paul Strand
- Edward S. Curtis
- Alvin Langdon Coburn
- Clarence H. White

Mounting Recommendations:
Board: Non-buffered cotton rag
Process: Use a sink mat if the print is mounted. If it is not mounted, use hinges. If the print is tipped into a book page, let it remain attached and mat it with non-buffered rag.

This photogravure was originally included in the March 2, 1914 issue of The Mentor, *a booklet issued semi-monthly by The Mentor Association of NY, NY*

PLATINUM PRINTS (PLATINOTYPE)

Years in Use: 1873 – Present

Overview: William Willus is commonly thought to be the inventor of the platinum or palladium print. The first patent was issued in 1873 and the last commercial production stopped in 1937. However, photographers have since started using the process again and the material is available. Platinum prints had tremendous tone range and were used by many of the Photo-Secessionists. The process became too expensive and was dropped. The process is considered by many to be the finest photographic image ever produced.

Identifying Characteristics:
- Normally silvery gray although other tones can be made such as sepia color.
- Large tonal range on emulsion. Even deep shadows have detail.
- Damages any paper near it causing a yellowing, catalystic image transfer. Check to see if it has been stored against another print or paper for a long period. There will be a reverse image burned into the other surface.
- Paper support is usually rag or cotton fiber paper.

Care & Handling: Platinum prints are very hardy and can be handled like a normal silver print. Platinum prints are being made again by artists and photographers. Be careful of these modern prints since they are hand-coated and much work goes into producing them. Unmounted prints may show physical damage such as acid burns, mildew, foxing and stains.

Possible Presentation Techniques:
- Mounted (early examples may be wet mounted, later examples dry mounted)
- Loose
- Tipped in

Some Photographers Using This Process:
- P. H. Emerson
- Frederick H. Evans
- A.L. Coburn
- Alfred Stieglitz
- Clarence White
- Edward Steichen

Paper which has been stored against a platinum print for a long period may have a reverse image of the print burned into it

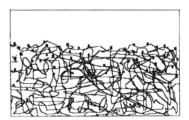

Profile of Platinum Print. The platinum image particles are suspended in the paper fibers of the substrate. Platinum prints are usually on rag or cotton fiber paper support.

Mounting Recommendations:
Board: Buffered or non-buffered, cotton rag board.
Process: Use hinges or corner or edge mounts. Since this print process is expensive and time-consuming, dry, wet, spray or pressure-sensitive mounting should be done only with a waiver from the customer.

POLAROID®

Years in Use: Polaroid Black & White 1948 – Present
Color 1965 – Present

Overview: Polaroid prints are not considered quite as stable as chromogenic prints. Be aware that the black and white Polaroid print must be coated as soon as it is completely processed. This coating should not be subjected to heat. All of the processing goes on in the film package so there may not be a negative available for more prints. The print is the original. There is one negative/positive Polaroid film available, which produces both a negative and a positive at the same time.

Identifying Characteristics:
- Black and white prints have to be coated once processed. This coating is quite thick and may show as brush strokes. Image degradation may show through the coating if the sealant is not applied evenly. Older prints will actually show image loss where the coating is incomplete.
- If the paper support is not trimmed, it will have a characteristic shape.
- Edge of print may show incomplete processing (uneven image).

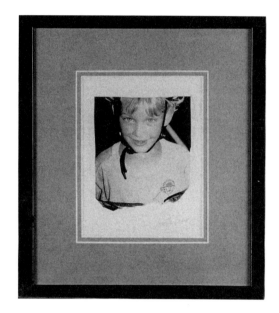

Polaroid transfer image to watercolor paper.

Possible Presentation Techniques:
A recent trend is to create a Polaroid transfer print by transferring the image and applying it to a second substrate. The new substrate is often rag, watercolor paper or cloth. The image looks off-color and is sometimes purposely distorted.
- Usually unmounted

Photographer Using This Process:
- Ansel Adams

Mounting Recommendations:
Board: Non-buffered cotton rag
Process: Use edge mounts or corner pockets.
Do not dry mount. Polaroid prints are very sensitive to heat.

Framing Recommendations:
Cover mats: Double mat
Glazing: UV

SALTED PAPER PRINTS

Years in Use: 1840–1870

Overview: Salted paper prints were used between 1840 to the late 1860s. Salted paper prints were silver and used to print Calotype negatives and later albumen on glass negatives before albumen prints were developed. It is often thought to be very soft focus material, but this was caused primarily by the paper negatives.

Identifying Characteristics:
- The print colors could vary from untoned (reddish-brown tint), to gold-toned (purple tint).
- Under a 30x magnification the paper fibers can be easily seen.
- The silver image will appear to be in the paper fibers and not on top of them.

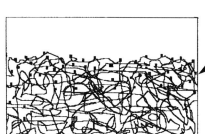

Profile of a Salted Paper Print.

Silver Fibers are Attached to Paper Fibers and are Mostly Near the Paper Surface.

Care & Handling: An older salted paper print can be over 150 years old and probably originated in England. It will be fragile and should be handled with extreme care. It is recommended that a paper conservator be used for consultation.

Possible Presentation Techniques:
- Mounted
- Loose
- Tipped in

Some Photographers Using This Process:
- Fox Talbot
- W. Langenheim
- F. Langenheim
- Henri le Secq
- David Octavius Hill
- Robert Adamson

Mounting Recommendations:
  Board: Buffered, cotton rag
  Process: If the print is unmounted, use hinges or corner and edge mounts if the substrate sturdy.

Framing Recommendations:
  Cover mats: double mat for unmounted prints
  Glazing: UV

Silver Developing-Out Gelatin Print

Years in Use: 1874 – Present

Overview: The paper is coated with a baryta layer which provides the whiteness and fills the fibers. The gelatin binder layer contains either silver bromide or silver chloride which is the sensitized image-making material. It is a developing-out process, which means that it must be exposed and then developed in chemistry to make the latent image visible. The paper may be either a fiber or a resin-coated substrate. The resin-coated, or RC paper (from 1968), does not last as long as a fiber-based material. Untoned, a fiber-based silver print should last at least 100 years. If it is toned, it can last up to 200 years. The RC paper lasts around 20 years.

Identifying Characteristics:
- No paper fibers will show under 30x inspection
- Most are black and white(monochrome). Some have been toned for color (black, brown, yellow, purple, etc.)

Care & Handling: Use white gloves when handling silver prints. Care should be taken to insure that the paper does not kink. This process is very stable and can withstand much display time.

Possible Presentation Techniques:
- Paper folder

Early versions may be mounted on:
- Carte-de-visite
- Cabinet card
- Stereograph
- Boudoir card
- Imperial card
- Minette card
- Panel
- Promenade card
- Victoria card
  (for actual card sizes, see page 89)
- Dry mounted (fine art photography)

Some Photographers Using This Process:
- Ansel Adams
- Helen Levitt
- Beaumont Newhall
- Alfred Stieglitz
- Edward Steichen

Mounting Recommendations:
Double-weight fiber prints will expand and contract in response to humidity and disconnect from the mat if not mounted well.
  Board: Non-buffered cotton rag
  Process: If the print is unsigned, it may be dry mounted. If it is signed, use hinges or a float mount

Framing Recommendations:
  Cover mats: Double mat
  Glazing: UV

Hand-Tinted Print
Monochrome prints may be hand-colored using pigments made specifically for photographic use.

Tintype (Ferrotype or Melainotype)

Years in Use: 1854–1930s

Overview: The tintype was invented by Adolph Alexandre Martin (French). The tintype was exposed directly in the camera and processed. There was no negative for additional prints. The tintype used the wet collodion emulsion. The tintype was very popular during the Civil War and did not die out until in the 1930s. Usually tintypes were portraits, but there are some rare outdoor scenes. The tintype was successful because it was so inexpensive to produce and could withstand harsh treatment, such as being sent through the mail. Many Civil War soldiers had their portraits taken in uniform to send to their families.

Identifying Characteristics:
- Attracted to a magnet.
- Coated on a brown or black lacquered (japanned) iron plate.
- Some were hand-tinted.
- May be clipped off on two or four corners
- Coated with a varnish which protected it from the environment.
- Flat muddy whites or highlights
- Usually they are well-worn, especially on the edges.
- May have been bent with rust may be forming under the emulsion.

Care & Handling: Cleaning a tintype can be done with a bath of mild soap and water, (Ivory Flakes® or similar). Dry the tintype with a hair dryer so that rust does not develop.

Possible Presentation Techniques:
- Cases
- Albums
- Paper envelopes
- Carte-de-visite
- Loose

Mounting Recommendations:
    Board: Non-buffered cotton rag
    Process: sink mat

Hand-Tinted Print
Monochrome prints may be hand-colored using pigments made specifically for photographic use.

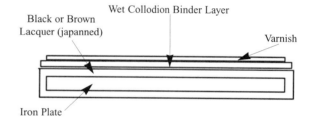

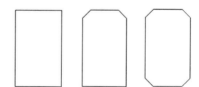

Typical shapes of tintypes.

Framing Photography 47

UltraStable Permanent Color

Years in Use: 1991 – Present

Overview: It was developed by Charles Berger and produces brilliant color. The process is a modernization of the old carbon process and, unlike other types of modern color prints, uses pigments rather than dyes. The process allows the printer to use any substrate. It is expected to last over 500 years. The cost is about $800 to $1000 to produce the first 16x20" print.

Identifying Characteristics:
- Because of high cost of this process, customers will be able to identify process.
- Matte surface.
- Coated on either high-quality paper or polyester substrate.
- Used primarily for portraiture and limited edition photography.
- Check image for registration of color.

Possible Presentation Techniques:
- Unmounted

Photographer Using This Process:
- Charles Berger

Mounting Recommendations:
    Board: Non-buffered cotton rag
    Process: Hinges using water-soluble adhesives

Framing Recommendations: This print will probably outlast the framing package several times over so depend on the shape of the mats, rather than color, to make an attractive mat design. The simpler the design, the better, so that it may withstand the change in trends and styles.
    Moulding: Aluminum or wood with a sealing material in the rabbet. Line the rabbet of a wood frame with Lineco's Frame Sealing Tape.
    Cover Mats: Cotton rag
    Filler Board: Several sheets of rag – no foam center
    Glazing: UV glass or acrylic (for large pieces)
    Dust Cover: Seal with acrylic using screws to hold in place.

This brilliant color print is a modern version of the old carbon process.

A long lasting image can be printed onto various substrates using pigments for permanency.

CHAPTER 3
CONSERVATION METHODS

Most photographs from the 18th century have been mounted in the form of carte-de-visite, etc. However, in the late 1800s and into the 20th century more paper prints have survived in folded paper photographic cases or unmounted. Because these are often historic records of family events and ancestors, care should be taken to insure that the photographs continue to survive long after framing.

Photography may have considerable value to the owner for sentiment or investment. Conservation framing methods will preserve the photograph in the best possible manner.

Photographic images are produced by chemical reactions and, in some cases, the reactions continue undetected because the chemicals are in constant flux. In fact some emulsions become chemically inert only when the last of the image has faded.

Due to the chemical make-up of photographs, attention must be paid to the materials, matboards and glazing used when framing a photograph.

Conservation framing for photography should provide:
- materials and methods which will not chemically react with the photographic emulsion
- glazing materials that will filter out ultraviolet light
- mounting techniques that will support and protect the print while being totally reversible.
- decorative elements that will have no impact on the chemical environment of the frame package.

Before choosing a conservation method, identification of the type of photograph should be determined. The *Time Line* on pages 12 and 13 and the *Identification Chart* on pages 18 and 19 will assist in determining the photographic process used. Check Chapter 2 for recommendations.

Glazing
Whenever possible Ultraviolet glazing should be used. If a photograph is worth framing it is worth saving from undue exposure to light.

Decorative Matting
Fine quality artist watercolors and inks may be used to add decoration to the mat.

> *Photographic images are produced by chemical reactions and, in some cases, the reactions continue undetected because the chemicals are in constant flux.*

> *Conservation framing for photography should provide materials and methods which will not chemically react with the photographic emulsion.*

Framing Photography 49

PAPER AND BOARDS

Both paper and boards are important to the preservation of the photographic image. Since the photograph may have been produced on or mounted onto cardboard and the framing will include some sort of backing board, matboard or mount board, the composition of boards is very important to framing photography.

Mat and mount boards are made from cotton or wood, which are the same materials used to make paper. Boards are simply layers of paper. Because cotton and wood must be processed before they are made into a paper or board, a framer needs to understand the chemical composition and ramifications of using different boards. The chemical composition of paper and boards will react with the chemical composition of a photograph.

BOARDS & BUFFERING

In the 1950s, a discovery was made highlighting the fact that papers which endured a long time were made using water with a high content of calcium carbonate. During the 1960s some board and paper manufacturers began to add calcium carbonate to their matboards. When calcium carbonate is added to the pulp mixture it attacks the "free-acids" – those below the neutral pH of 7. The term "acid-free" is now used to describe boards which have had this treatment as well as items that never had acid in them. Some companies now refer to their boards as buffered acid-free as opposed to naturally free of acids.

The buffering is helpful in extending the life of the board but how long depends on what type of pulp has been used in the original product. If it is cotton -- it will last with or without buffering; if it is highly processed alpha cellulose wood pulp, buffering creates neutral pH and has proven to last. However, if it is put into ground wood paper pulp, the buffer may be overpowered by the slowly increasing activity of the acid and eventually the board becomes acidic. The breakdown or hydrolysis can not be stopped, just slowed. This may take years or decades depending on the environment and other conditions.

Groundwood board which has been treated with calcium carbonate should not be used for mounting photographs. The calcium carbonate only extends the life of the board and does not provide the long-term mounting board required for a photograph that should last for generations.

The chemical composition of paper and boards will react with the chemical composition of a photograph.

The calcium carbonate functions as a buffering agent which neutralizes the acid created from the action of light, oxygen and moisture on the wood pulp.

Wood contains a material called lignin which, in its natural state, binds the cellulose fibers together. This material is made up of linked sugar molecules (polysaccharides). Cellulose is made of long chains of the same sugar molecules. Lignin is made of shorter chains of various types of sugar molecules which have the tendency to break, thus freeing protons. Lignin molecule chains break down into shorter chains and one proton is freed from each break. As these protons are freed, they start a chain reaction which results in a rise in the acidity of the paper. The protons start a chain reaction causing the breakdown of the cellulose, which results in smaller and weaker links seen as brittle and yellowed board.

Initially, rag paper was made of cotton scraps. This type of paper has lasted several hundred years. Most rag boards are no longer made of cotton scraps since the demand is high and the sources for pure cotton scraps is rare. Instead, paper manufacturers buy cotton linters directly from cotton processors. Natural cotton is roughly 90% pure cellulose when it is picked. There may be a minute amount of lignin that may come from a piece of leaf or stem on the cotton plant as it is harvested. However, that is completely removed with washing. Wood plants have a high content of lignin which can be as much as 30% of the total composition. The cellulose content in wood is about 50 to 60%. Lignin is removed from ground wood pulp with chemical and mechanical processing.

Boards produced with cotton are almost 98% pure alpha cellulose. Alpha cellulose is the term used to describe the long chain of sugar molecules that is needed for the production of fine paper and matboards. Pure cellulose, or alpha cellulose, is similar regardless from which plant it is extracted. So the strength and stability of wood or cotton alpha cellulose is similar.

The purity of the matboard cannot be totally guaranteed since neutralizing and washing paper fibers does not insure total absence of unwanted chemicals such as bleaches, sizing etc. Photographers have long been plagued with the problem of washing paper prints to rid them of chemicals that would later cause staining or image loss. The cellulose fibers provide dense clumped areas where chemicals can be found even after washing.

Cotton has only about 10% of impurities to eliminate but wood has between 40 and 50%. In addition, cotton is an annually renewable plant, while wood takes a very long time to renew.

Only the rag board comes in a non-buffered variety. Alpha cellulose made from wood must be buffered to be acid neutral, whereas cotton does not need buffering because it is naturally neutral.

Based on current studies and information, non-buffered rag should be used when placed directly against the following photographic emulsions: gelatin, albumen, chromogenic color, Ilfochrome Classics(Cibachrome), dye transfers, and cyanotypes. (Since buffering agents do not "migrate" from matboards, buffered mats can be used safely in the framing package, as long as a non-buffered board is used for the mat that actually touches the photo emulsion.) A buffered rag may be used directly on collodion, platinum, or platinum toned salted prints.

Premounted card photographs should be mounted onto buffered rag using a sink mount, as long as the emulsion does not actually touch the board. If the window mat touches the emulsion, a non-buffered board should be used to act as a barrier between the emulsion and the outer window mats.

If color requirements demand the use of wood alpha cellulose matboards near the emulsion, use them only with non-buffered rag barrier mats. It is not recommended to place wood alpha cellulose boards directly against photographic emulsions because of the buffering agent and the possibility of bleaching contaminants. If this must be done, a signed waiver of the use of conservation materials should be obtained from the customer prior to any work on the photograph.

Hinges

For paper substrate photographic prints, the museum hinge made out of mulberry tissue applied with cooked rice or wheat starch adhesive would be appropriate. With a polyester substrate or similar material, the use of an adhesive-bearing tape such as Filmoplast P 90 would be appropriate. Care should be taken to insure that the moisture of the starch adhesive never touches the emulsion surface.

A variation of the hinge is the technique called "pockets and suspenders", wherein the best of two worlds has been combined. Two hinges are used on the top while two mylar or polyester corner pockets are used at the bottom.

The pockets should be positioned so the print is not grounded against the bottom or side edge of the pocket. The pocket is only there to stop the pendulum effect. The hinge is actually the only support given to the print.

Using only the hinges produces a pendulum effect if the frame is moved roughly or is accidentally stored on its side.

If undue pressure is exerted on one of the hinges, the hinge will tear instead of the art because the mulberry tissue is thinner than the paper substrate. The pocket should stop the photograph from the pendulum effect which should prevent the hinge from tearing in the first place.

Museum or conservation hinging has to be done carefully since water-soluble adhesives are being used near the photographic emulsion. Some emulsions (such as albumen) crack when they are moistened and dried again. Others, like gelatin, soften when wet and then harden when dry. While wet they can be easily damaged, especially if the emulsion is under pressure against another surface or it picks up dirt.

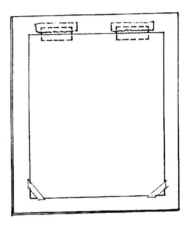

Pockets and Suspenders

To hinge paper based prints:
- *Hinges are torn from Japanese paper*
- *Paste is applied to the torn strips*
- *Pastes are:*
- *Cooked wheat or rice starch*
- *Zen Paste® by Archival Products, LA (already prepared wheat starch)*
- *Methyl cellulose paste*
- *Insta Hinges® Archival Products LA (ready-prepared Japanese paper with starch paste)*

The T-Hinge

1. Hand-tear the hinges to provide a gradual thickening of the hinge. The torn fibers spread out and provide a slope from the edges toward the center of the hinge, which prevents a sharp impression on the surface of the photo. A sharp impression may be created by a hinge with a cut edge.

2. Apply starch adhesive to no more than 1/8" of the hinge.

3. Attach one-half of the hinge to the front, top edge of the photograph and the other half to the backing board.

4. Place hinges on a flat surface with blotters and 2" squares of DuPont Tyvek® mylar or Seal Release Paper® placed on the top and bottom of the hinge to insure rapid drying and not scratch the surface of the art.

5. Place a piece of glass across the top of the print to keep the print flat. Make sure to cover all of the hinges while drying takes place.

6. Once dried, attach the hinge to the backing board with a cross-strip of mulberry paper. Use the blotter and Tyvek squares. Place the hinge at the top of the print paper so that as little of the print as possible is actually affected.

7. Place the glass back on the print to keep the print flat during the drying period. Make sure to cover all of the hinges at the same time.

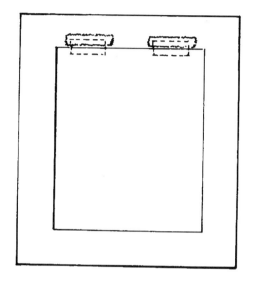

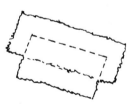

Use Filmoplast P 90 paper tape for polyester substrate photographs. Even though it violates the conservation standard of no self-adhesives, it is just about the only thing that will stick to the polyester photographs if a hinge is needed.

Float Hinges

The V-Hinge
Float hinges allow all of the art, including its edges, to be visible in the framing. The V-hinge is appropriate for smaller pieces. Hand-tear the hinges to provide a gradual thickening of the hinge. The torn fibers spread out and provide a slope which prevents a sharp impression on the surface.

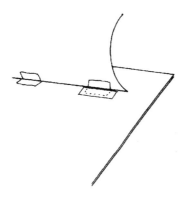

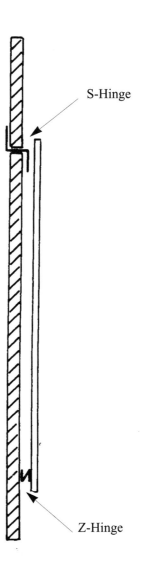

S-Hinge

Z-Hinge

The S-Hinge
The S-hinge, or pass-through hinge, will hold larger pieces securely. Use the mat cutter to cut slits in the board. Slip the hinge material through the slit. Attach the hinge to the photo on the back, top most edge.

The Z-Hinge
The Z-hinge is used to gently hold the lower part of a flopping photograph that may have been hinged at the top allowing the bottom edge to lift away from the backing board.

Take a small strip of hinging material and fold it into a "z". Attach one flat end to the photograph and the other to the backing board.

CORNER MOUNTS AND EDGE MOUNTS

To physically mount a photograph that has not been pre-mounted, the use of corner pockets or edge mounts is appropriate. Corner pockets used to be made from black paper before the effect of acidic paper was noted. The commercially-made corner mount has been greatly improved by using mylar or polyester materials.

Besides being used in albums, these mounts can be used for framing. They can be hidden behind the window mat.

Handmade corner mounts can be made from mulberry tissue and are superior since the mount strip is hand-torn allowing the fibers to fan out, providing a gentle slope from the surface of the mount to the photograph. Commercial corner mounts are stamped or cut with a sharp edge and can leave pressure or abrasive marks on the photographic emulsion.

The edge mount is similar to a corner mount except the mount is applied along the edges of the print and not the corner. These can also be handmade using mulberry tissue. There are also commercial versions, but the edges are sharp. Commercial mounts can be altered by lining them with hand-torn mulberry tissue, thus softening the sharp edges.

Corner and edge mounts should not be used with photographs over the size of 11x14". A larger photograph may settle under its own weight and begin to sag in the middle, causing slight waves in the paper.

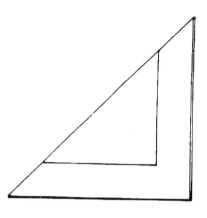

Corner Mount

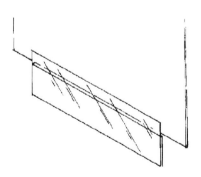

Edge Mount

Framing Photography 55

SINK MATS

The sink mat is perhaps the best way to frame a carte-de-visite or cabinet photograph. Careless physical examination by the viewer can quickly destroy the photographic package.

To help slow the action of the acidic breakdown of the card, use a lignin-free, buffered cotton or rag board fro the sink mat.

1. Measure the item to be framed.

2. Cut a window mat 1/8" smaller than the item so it will overlap.

3. Set the item in the center of the backing board. measure the space from the item to the edge of the backing board and cut strips of rag to completely fill the space. Allow the item no more than 1/8" extra space.

4. Layer strips of rag to reach the same height as the photograph. The strips may be held together with white glue or double-sided tape.

5. Set a window mat on top of the stack and place the package in the frame. The window mat may be attached to the stack with glue or double-sided tape.

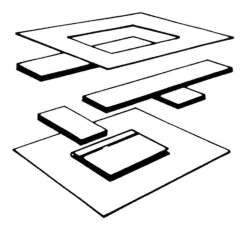

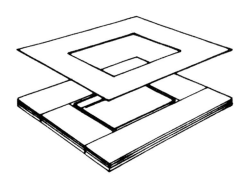

Chapter 4
Mounting Methods
Dry Mounting

The dry mounting technique should only be used for unmounted, modern gelatin or chromogenic color prints which are not signed or numbered as a limited edition.

This process is *not recommended for old photographs*, photographic limited editions, glossy Ilfochrome Classic (Cibachrome) prints, Polaroid prints, platinum or other non-silver prints because:
- Most of these prints are valuable to a varying degree.
- Some prints such as the Polaroid print cannot withstand a heated press.
- The dry mounting process is not completely reversible. When reversing is attempted, damage and residue may result.

Most photographic emulsions are chemical coatings that are primarily made of gelatin (animal bones, hides, etc.), and albumen (egg whites). There are some conservators that have shown concern regarding animal products being stored in buffered enclosures. There are non-buffered mounting boards available, but consider the hardness and surface texture before settling on a specific board to use. A board that is as smooth as possible and fairly hard is recommended. The board must be strong enough to provide good support for the photograph.

Seal Colormount® tissue provides good protection for modern gelatin, black and white and chromogenic color photographs. It does not require high temperatures to activate the tissue. This is especially important for color emulsions.

The use of a mechanical dry mount press allows a print that is larger than the press to be mounted. The heat vacuum press can only mount up to the size for which it is built. Temperatures above 205°F should not be used. More time in the press instead of higher temperature is better.

Recommendations for Dry Mounting Photographs

PHOTOGRAPHS	YES	NO	DOCUMENTED PHOTOGRAPHERS' PREFERENCE
Unsigned black & white (Modern silver gelatin)	X		
Unsigned platinum		X (1)	
Antique		X (1)	
Limited edition prints		X (1)	X (2)*
Unsigned Chromogenic color	X		
Polaroid		X (1)	
Oil- or water-colored &/or toned unsigned modern black & white	X (3)		
Oil- or water-colored &/or toned signed modern black & white		X (1)	X (2)*
Prints with no negatives available		X (1)	X (2)*
Unsigned prints with negatives available	X		
Unsigned, retouched black & white toned or untoned	X		
Prints used for display advertising	X (4)		
Hand-coated emulsions		X (1)	X (2)*
Multiple, painted photographic prints spliced together (such as panoramic prints)		X (1)	X (2)*
Computer generated electronic Images		X (5)	

(1) Use conservation techniques.
(2) If the photographer has provided a signed mounting instruction for the specific print, use the technique unless conservation guidelines are violated, then obtain a written waiver if you prefer not to follow the photographer's directions.
(3) |Best if mounted prior to oil or water coloring.
(4) Not to be considered for a limited edition or original. If there is a hint of this possibility then revert to conservation techniques or obtain a waiver from the photographer.
(5) Some works are heat-sensitive. Heat may cause ink binder to melt and transfer or distort image.
* The photography industry used to consider dry mounting appropriate, however, the museums now consider dry mounting to be harmful and detrimental to the longevity of the photograph.

Framing Photography 57

Use a sheet of scrap matboard just below the platen, then a piece of release paper, and finally the photograph and mounting board. The scrap matboard serves the following purposes:
- It insures that the surface on which the photographic print is being placed is always clean and smooth.
- It keeps the edge of the platen from leaving a mark on the surface of the print.
- It diffuses the heat to insure that the print gets even heat and does not allow scorching.

Discard the scrap matboard when it gets dirty. A mat with one side covered with release paper can be purchased or self-made. If the board and the release tissue are used separately, then only one has to be discarded when it is dirty.

1. Cut a piece of mounting board 2" larger than the size of the completed project.

Note: Use a non-buffered or buffered rag or alpha cellulose board for mounting. The support paper substrate of the photograph separates and protects the buffer sensitive emulsion from the mounting board.

2. Cut a piece of dry mounting tissue 1" larger than the frame.

3. Lay the photograph face down on a hard surface. Tack the tissue to the print on the top edge using a tacking iron and release paper.

4. Place the print face up into position on the mounting board.

5. Hold the tacked edge while carefully bending the bottom edge up and tack the tissue to the mounting board.

6. Place in heat mounting press. Follow manufacturers' instructions regarding time and temperature. The layer of chemicals that make up a photograph is delicate. Excessive pressure on the surface may leave a mark.

7. Remove from press and allow to cool.
Using a knife such as the X-Acto #1, trim the excess dry mount tissue from around the print. A lot of pressure is not required. Slowly draw the knife down for a stable, straight cut line. Make sure the tissue and the print are laying flat and do not move while they are being cut.

Foam center boards should not be used for dry mounting. They are soft and can be easily dented by pressure.

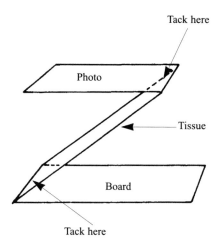

Z-Tack Method

Note: Keep the area under the print clean and free of dust while dry mounting. A small amount of compressed air can be used to blow the dust particles from the mounting board, print and the tissue. Any dirt specks will be noticeable after dry mounting, especially if the surface is glossy. If that happens and the print is a color print for display, with the customer's approval, spray the print with Sureguard McDonald Pro-Tecta-Cote Matte spray. Not only will the spray make the bump on the surface almost disappear, it will also help protect the print from ultraviolet light. Spraying a photograph is not considered conservation method because it does change the photograph irreversibly.

Do not cut the mount board to the final size until the cover mats have been cut. Once the cover mats are cut, they are a perfect guide for cutting the mount board. Lay the mat package on top of the print and get it perfectly aligned.

Run a pencil around the mat package leaving a line on the mounting board. Use a mat cutter to cut the mounting board down to final size. If the cut is made on the inside of the pencil line, it cancels out the width of the pencil and the final board is quite accurate.

Any dirt specks will be noticeable after dry mounting, especially if the surface is glossy.

Dwell time: the span of time a mounting package remains under pressure either in a press or under a weight.

Open time: period of time during which an adhesive is workable, allowing repositioning and smoothing.

Pressure-Sensitive Mounting

Pressure-sensitives are adhesives that bond with pressure. They are typically coated with release papers which protect the adhesives from bonding until needed. Some adhesives are more aggressive than others. Check manufacturers' instructions. Pressure sensitive adhesives such as Perfect Mount® by Crescent require 8 to 24 hours to create a bond, because the adhesive is intentionally "dry" to provide an opportunity for repositioning the photograph to achieve the exact correct position.

Some pressure-sensitive adhesives do not work well with double-weight papers, because the adhesives are not strong enough and the photographic paper pulls itself from the surface of the mount board. Pressure sensitives should not be used on anything but unsigned chromogenic prints and possibly the newer electronic copies which are often heat and moisture sensitive.

Most pressure-sensitive boards have adhesives covered with protective release paper which is removed prior to mounting. These are available as double-sided sheets of film and as a board with one surface coated with adhesive. Perfect Mount Film and Perfect Mount Board are acid-free and will not discolor. However, the adhesive becomes permanent as it ages, so it would not be appropriate for antique prints or fine art photography.

Pressure sensitives should not be used on anything but unsigned chromogenic prints and possibly the newer electronic copies which are often heat and moisture sensitive.

PRESSURE-SENSITIVE MOUNTING

1. Clean dust from photograph.

2. To begin, start at corner and use a fingernail to carefully lift the release paper to expose the adhesive. Take care not to separate the adhesive layer from the board.

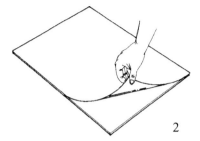

Note: Do not touch the adhesive with hand, as oil from fingers will inhibit adhesion.

3. Pull back the release paper, exposing an edge of adhesive. Place the photo on the exposed edge. Carefully pull the release paper from under the item, allowing the work to sit on the adhesive surface.

4. Position and reposition the photograph until it is in the desired position. A board which is larger than the photograph may be used and trimmed after mounting.

5. Check for air bubbles by holding the piece up to the light and inspecting the surface. Remove air bubbles by repositioning the piece.

6. Once the photograph is in the desired position, set the release paper on the face of the item to avoid scratching the surface. Apply firm, even pressure with a plastic squeegee or burnisher. A mounting press may also be used (no heat necessary).

7. Store the finished piece flat for a minimum of 24 hours to allow the adhesive to cure.

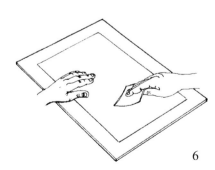

Framing Photography

Wet Mounting

Take great care when wet mounting a photograph because water spotting and paste migration may ruin a photograph emulsion.

Wet mounting is the oldest method of adhering paper to a backing board. Wet mounting uses wet glues and pastes, it requires little financial investment and it may be completed by hand with only a weight for pressure. It is a good alternative technique for oversized items when equipment size limitations are an issue.

The process, though economical, may be time-consuming and messy. The permanency of successful wet mountings is often directly related to operator ability to properly apply an even layer of adhesive, allowing for appropriate dwell time, and adequate weight during drying. Thus, the largest variable when using wet glues involves the application of adhesive, followed closely by the elements of time and pressure. Use of a cold vacuum press will increase the permanency by creating a stronger original bond.

A thick paste or liquid adhesive must be evenly applied to the substrate prior to positioning. The three elements of mounting to be controlled during wet mounting are time, pressure and moisture. Temperature only becomes an issue when attempting to apply adhesives in an extremely hot, humid or cold environment which might affect the flow and/or drying time of the selected adhesive.

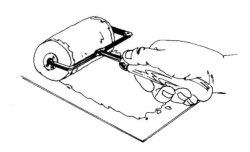

Standard Wet Mounting

1. Begin with a dollop of paste on a piece of scrap glass, then roll a brayer across to even out the adhesive. It is not recommended to use matboard scraps in place of the glass because they will absorb the moisture from the paste. This absorption accelerates drying and cuts down on working time.

2. Apply adhesive to the substrate rather than the print or photograph. Stiffness of the mounting board tolerates the roller better than the print or photograph. Make certain the glue is evenly applied and covers every square inch of board.

3. Align the print with the substrate across the top edge. Tack the print by sliding gently from the top to the bottom – first down the center, then to the edges, respectively.

4. Check alignment to mount board; dwell time will allow for corrections if necessary .

5. Cover the print with a sheet of clean kraft paper or release paper and gently brayer from the center to the edges to remove air bubbles.

6. Let the project dry under weight (a lite of glass will do) for 4-24 hours for the most permanent bond. Do not flex the project to reflatten until total bond time has been achieved.

Spray Mounting

Spray mounting is not recommended for valued photographs. Spray mounting is an inexpensive alternative, but does not ensure long-term permanence. It requires no equipment—though a spray booth and/or ventilation hood is highly recommended—and needs to be weighted while drying.

Permanence of spray mounting will increase with the use of a cold vacuum press. A suitable bond is more difficult to achieve in high humidity.

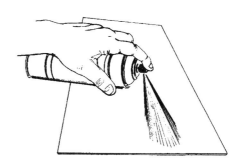

The three basic elements to address with spray mounting are time (both open and bond time), pressure and moisture. Adequate time after applying the spray is required for the solvent to evaporate and the adhesive to become tacky. This is when the print may be aligned and repositioned if necessary, and is known as "open time". Though the initial bond is made within the first hour, pressure is required for 4-24 hours for the most permanent bond.

Spray Mounting a Photograph

1. Cover work surface with kraft paper or newsprint to absorb test sprays and oversprays.

2. Fold pieces of kraft paper into long tent shapes to keep the photograph from slipping onto the overspray.

3. Lay the photograph to be mounted face down on the tents.

4. Shake the spray can well and do a test spray to make sure the can is working properly. Check the manufacturer's recommendations to determine the ideal spraying distance between the spray can nozzle and the photograph.

5. Begin to spray adhesive from the top and spray in rows to the bottom. Overspraying on the top, bottom and sides will insure that the adhesive covers the edges.

Note: Make sure to spray the adhesive evenly and thoroughly. Every inch of the photograph must be covered with adhesive.

6. Spray a second coat of adhesive in the opposite direction of the first coat so that the rows crisscross.

7. Let the adhesive sit for 15-30 seconds so that it gets tacky.

8. Position the print on the substrate.

9. Cover with a release paper and smooth from the center to the edges using a flat hand or soft brayer.

10. Set flat under weight for extended time to allow the adhesive to dry and bond.

11. Invert can and clear nozzle of remaining spray after use.

STATIC MOUNTING

by Paul MacFarland, CPF

Static mounting is useful for polyester-based photographs such as Ilfochrome Classics® or computer-generated art. These high gloss ultra-smooth images resist mounting adhesives, and suffer from "orange peel" effect when mounted to most substrates. When hinged, the center of a plastic-based image often bows outward toward the glazing, creating an irregular surface, distorting the image, and often making contact with the glazing. The static mounting method uses a sheet of acrylic for the mounting surface. The artwork is held in place by a combination of a static charge and photo corners or perimeter mounting flanges.

Materials:
    Sheet of acrylic
    Photo

1. Cut a sheet of acrylic to the frame rabbet dimension, leaving the cover sheets on the acrylic.

2. Use a T-square and pencil to measure and mark opening to accommodate photo. Add an extra 1/4" to opening for leeway.

3. Cut along the marking with a sharp utility knife; do not remove the cover sheet yet.

4. Prepare for mounting the artwork by having an assistant(s) hold the artwork by the edges, gently bowing the artwork into a "U" shape.

5. Peel up an edge of the cover sheet, just enough to firmly grasp it.

6. Quickly rip the cover sheet away to create as much static charge as possible and immediately place the artwork, center first, onto the acrylic sheet. A light downward pressure on the "U"-shaped artwork will allow the center to attach first, followed by the edges. *This can only be attempted once.*

7. The artwork should now be held in place by the static charge which will keep the center from bowing outward, but, to be safe, the edges should be attached with perimeter mounts, such as Lineco See-Thru Mounting Strips®.

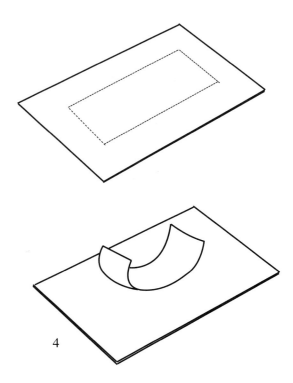

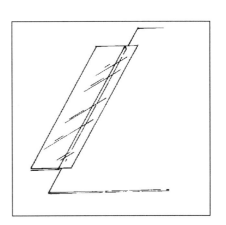

CHAPTER 5
PROJECTS

SINK MAT BUILT AROUND PHOTOGRAPHS & FOLDERS

Project 1

Many folders from the early 20th century through the 1930s are quite beautiful and should be allowed to be viewed. The photographs were attached to the folders by the photographer, so if possible the folder should be left intact.

Buffered matboards and UV filtering glass should be used. In this project, each folder is supported in its own sink mat. To keep the old folders from breaking at the seams when folded backwards, cut a piece of buffered rag matboard slightly smaller than the length and width of the folder and fold the flaps over this piece of board to cushion the seams in the framing package. The gentle support provided by the sink mat also helps to minimize pressure on the folder.

The pressure of the back-folded folder forces the photo towards the glass. A double mat thickness is required to keep the photo from touching the glass.

Full support and pressure must be maintained between the glass and the top mat; the narrow strip of matting between the photos helps accomplish this. To show that the two photos belong together, a small section of the center strip was removed and ink lines were added to tie the design together.

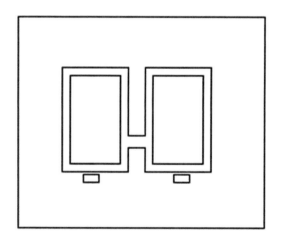

Slip a piece of cotton rag in between the back-folded flaps to keep them from folding too flat and cracking.

Framing Photography 65

Framing a Mounted Photograph

Project 2

Many old photos are already mounted to a decorative board or decorative folder. If the board is sturdy enough and flat enough, it can be placed in a frame without matting. The photo must be kept from touching the glass.

1. Line the rabbet of the frame with Lineco Frame Sealing Tape to reduce acid migration from the wood.

2. Use spacer such as Econospace or FrameSpace, which attaches to the glass. This will keep the photo from touching the glass, allowing proper air circulation within the frame job.

Project 3

Newer photos can also be framed without matting.

1. Dry mount the photograph to a 4-ply buffered rag board. Note: Use a pressure sensitive mounting method if the photo is heat sensitive.

2. Line the rabbet of the built frame with Lineco Frame Sealing Tape.

3. Cut glass and apply Framespace to the edges.

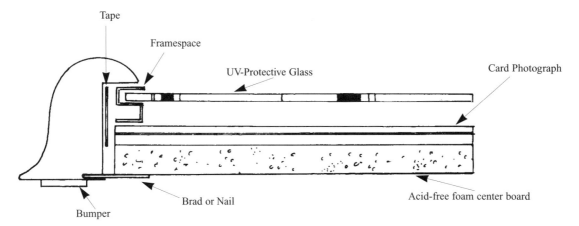

66 Framing Photography

DISPLAY CASE FOR A PHOTOGRAPHIC ALBUM

Project 4

This consists of a flat-style base frame that the album will set on, and a removable cover with a glass face to protect the album while still allowing it to be viewed. The cover sets on the outer edge of the base frame.

Mouldings: Larson-Juhl X2380 and X2383
Matboards: Crescent PhotoRag and Moorman Suede

1. Build the base (see illustration at bottom of page.)

2. Fit suede board and foam center board into base.

3. Attach bumpers to all four corners of base, to protect the surface it will rest on.

4. Build cover (lid) to rest on base.

5. Cut two identical mats to fit lid. Use unbuffered rag for the undermat. The top mat may be unbuffered or buffered rag. The top mat may be cut to feature a photograph. Black and white copies on fiber paper should be used for longevity.

6. Place the mats back to back. Fit into the lid along with a piece of UV filtering glass, using stained balsa wood strips to hold everything in place with a nicely finished appearance.

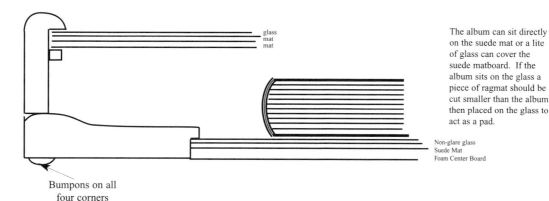

The album can sit directly on the suede mat or a lite of glass can cover the suede matboard. If the album sits on the glass a piece of ragmat should be cut smaller than the album then placed on the glass to act as a pad.

Framing Photography

Building a Glass Box with an Easel for Card Photographs

Project 5

First build an easel using moulding and Rabbetspace. (See Project 13.)

BUILDING THE GLASS BOX

1. Cut four pieces of UV filtering glass about 2" taller than the height of the card photograph when standing on easel, and wide enough for an easy fit on all sides of the photo, without risk of the photo accidentally touching the glass. Using production stops will provide the most consistent results.

2. Clean glass and smooth edges.

3. Using 3/8" copper tape, tape all four edges of each glass plate. Smooth out tape with flat bone or similar tool.

Note: Do not breathe solder fumes while soldering. Wear protective gloves.

4. Run a light coating of water-soluble flux only on the outer edge. Heat will make the flux run to the remainder of the tape and clean the surface. If it does not, then a little flux added with a brush will solve the problem. Flux will help the solder cover the surface of the tape. Remember, the more flux that is put on the more that will have to be cleaned off later.

Note: The best solder for this type of work is 50/50 solder. This may be found at stained glass stores. Use a 100-watt soldering iron which may also be found at stained glass stores. After the iron is hot, clean the end. (Ask the dealer how to tin the iron tip before starting a project.) This is done by rubbing the end (while hot) on a wet sponge and then placing some solder on the tip.

5. Run the iron along the top edge (where the flux is) and the solder should flow out onto the tape. Once the top edge is done, start on the sides, one side at a time. Add additional solder as needed. Do not try to build up a lot of solder on the tape.

6. Clean the glass and the solder with glass cleaner.

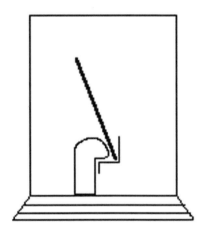

68 *Framing Photography*

7. Using a moulding corner vise, tack the ends of the glass plates together to form the box. Tack only on the outside. The glass may not always touch at all points—this is fine.

8. Measure the top of the box and cut glass to fit. This piece of glass should sit on top of the side pieces. Tape and tin as before. Tack solder the top onto the glass box.

9. Run a second layer of tape over areas that have been tacked, to hide the seams and straighten out any uneven edges on the first tape. This tape also adds strength to the box. Do not apply tape inside the box, just on the outside.

10. Add some flux to the new tape and tin. Fill in around the tape edges so that the new tape blends in with the first layer.

11. Use glass cleaner to completely clean the box.

12. The solder can be chemically etched to a black or dark color that looks like an antique brass edge. Be careful using the etching fluid or paste. Read and follow the instructions. After etching the solder, clean the box with water and then glass cleaner.

13. After the glass box is complete, build a frame base to fit, and attach easel to base (see Project 13.) Set photo on easel, then set glass box on the base.

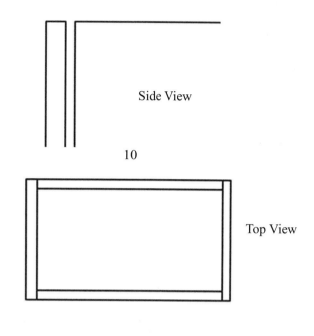

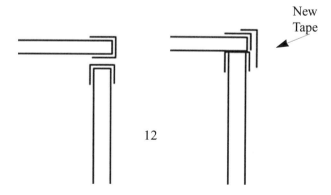

Framing Photography 69

Union or Moroccan Case

Project 6

This can be done to any cased image (ie., daguerreotype, tintype, ambrotype or paper print). The rods support the case with gentle pressure from all sides. The mirror at the back of the frame package allows the reverse side of the case to be seen.

Materials:
- Buffered rag mats
- Clear acrylic rods (from hobby shops or plastic suppliers) or brass rods
- UV-protective glass
- Mirror
- Double-sided tape

1. Cut top mat (a double mat) with 1-3/8" and 1-3/4" borders.

2. Cut several spacer mats. Two or three of these will be cut in parts to make slots to accommodate the height and width of the rods. These slotted mats should be sandwiched between whole spacer mats to create a well-supported package.

3. Attach rods to mat with double-sided tape. Rods should be cut to fit firmly between case and frame rabbet. Place double-sided tape in slots and insert rods in place. Once inserted they will stay in place. A variation can be done with brass or copper rods or tubing, coated with a sealer to protect the finish.

Moulding: Larson Juhl X460
Matboard: Crescent 1105 Rag

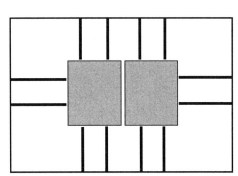

Rods reach from edge of case to the inside edge of the frame.

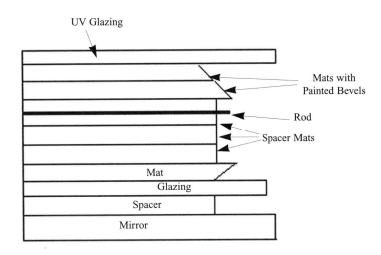

70 *Framing Photography*

A Carte-de-Visite with a Civil War Stamp

Project 7

This framing allows both sides of the card to be viewed. Since a carte-de-visite is mounted on an old paper matboard, which is highly acidic, it should be protected with buffered rag or alpha cellulose mats.

1. Cut top mat with a 2-3/8" margin on the top and sides and 2-1/2" margin on the bottom. Cut a second mat with a 2-5/8" margin on the top and sides and a 3" margin on the bottom. Cut additional window mats for each of the top mats, proportioning to make a balanced design, with the innermost mat openings sized to slightly overlap the carte-de-visite.

2. Cut a two-ply rag sink mat to closely fit the carte-de-visite.

3. Put the two top mats back-to-back with the two-ply sink mat containing the carte-de-visite sandwiched between them.

4. Place a piece of UV protective glass on both sides and place the mat package in the frame.

5. Since this framing is intended for viewing from both sides, use Rabbetspace to fit the package into the frame. Miter the rabbetspace for a clean fit, then place bumpers over the miters to finish.

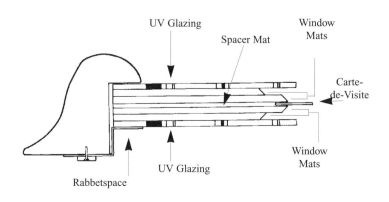

Framing Photography

Framing a Card Photograph and its Original Frame

Project 8

This framing allows the photo to be used with its original frame, while also protecting the photo from acid damage caused by the old framing materials.

1. Restore and clean the original frame. Line the inside of the original frame with Frame Sealing Tape made by Lineco, or a similar tape.

2. Cut a new mat of buffered rag to fit the old frame. Cut a sink mat to closely fit the card photograph. Add a buffered rag backing board, and fit this mat package into the old frame.

3. Attach this entire package into a shadowbox. Fit UV filtering glass and window mats into new frame. Line the interior of the shadowbox with foam center board covered with matboard. For added dimension, raise the old frame package with a spacer mat so it appears to float above the backing board.

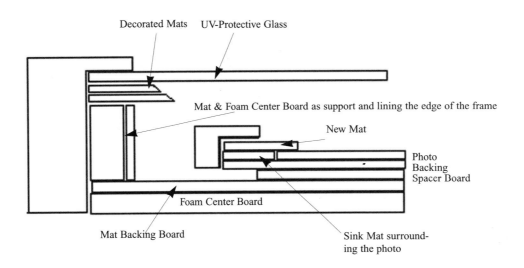

72 *Framing Photography*

Framing Two Moroccan Cases

Project 9

This framing will work with any cased image (ie., tintype, daguerreotype, ambrotype or paper print.) Use unbuffered rag matboards wherever boards will touch the leather case.

1. Cut top mat with 3" margin. Paint bevel and add marblized paper panel and ink lines.

2. Cut 2 or 3 spacer mats. One mat should be cut in parts so that pieces can extend to the cases and a long segment can be added between the cases. This will provide stable support for the uneven objects and make the mats look square. Attach these "suspension" pieces to the spacer mats with double-sided tape.

4. Support cases against the backing board by running cotton thread lightly around the hinge and the hooks.

Moulding: Larson Juhl X460
Matboard: Crescent 1630 and 2297

Pieces of matboard push towards the case to hold it in place.

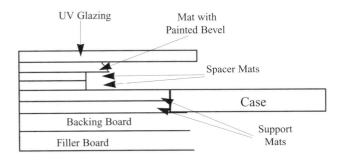

Framing Photography 73

A Hinged-Cover Door Frame

Project 10A

This framing package helps protect a historical photograph that is beginning to show image loss. Since it should not be displayed, except during actual viewing, this frame has a cover door that is hinged to the main frame. The door can hold a copy of the original or a description of the photograph inside.

The protected photograph is mounted in a sink mat in the main frame with non-buffered cotton rag mat and UV protective glass. The items in the door frame are a newspaper article and a photograph of a railroad pass. The newsprint has been treated with calcium carbonate and the photograph is on fiber paper. Both are dry mounted.

Moulding: Artisan
Matboard: Crescent Archival PhotoRag Board

This is the door frame with the newsprint and railroad pass.

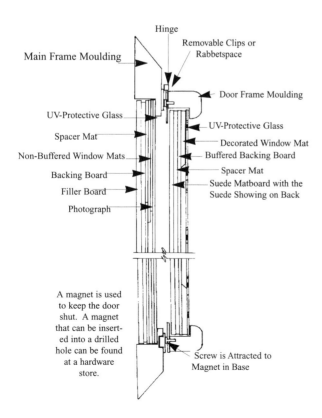

This is the inner frame with the valuable original photograph.

74 *Framing Photography*

Card Photograph in a Hinged-Door Frame

Project 10B

A hinged door and frame provides protection and easy access to the photograph. For maximum protection from light damage, a copy of the photograph could be matted and placed in the door.

1. Build base frame and door frame. Fit glass and boards into base frame. Fit UV filtering glass in the door frame.

2. Silicone a piece of suede board or buffered rag on the front side of the back glass. This provides a cushion backdrop for the photograph. Allow the silicone to cure completely.

3. To create a support for the card photograph, use two pieces of moulding about 3" long. Attach Rabbetspace to the inside rabbet of each piece of moulding. Position the supports on the glass to gently but securely hold the card photograph. Attach the moulding to the glass with silicone. Let the silicone cure completely.

4. Place the card photograph in the slots. The card photograph can be easily removed if necessary.

5. Use two hinges and a magnet catch to attach the door to the frame.

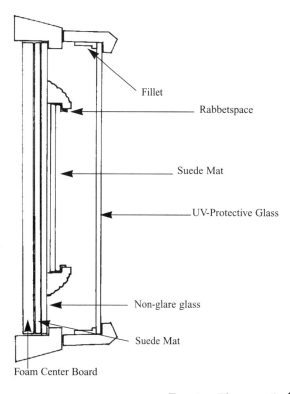

Framing Photography

Uncased Ambrotype, Tintype or Daguerreotype
in a Preserver

Project 11

The print shown here is still in its preserver but without its case. The preserver may be uneven but is often beautiful enough to be displayed.

The support is made from strips of matboard that are attached to the underside of the window mat. The strips should be positioned to gently press against the uneven preserver. The result is an open sink mat. The glass touches the preserver and keeps it in place.

All mats should be buffered.

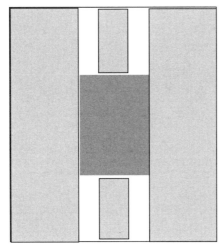

Light gray areas are pieces of matboard used to wedge the case in position.

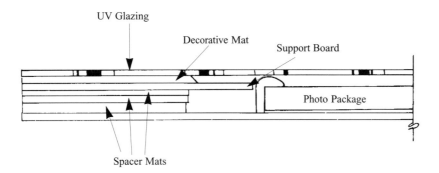

76 *Framing Photography*

TABLE TOP DISPLAY CASE

Project 12

Support mount made from brass sheets allows a case with a broken hinge to be displayed as it originally looked.

This box serves as a cover to protect the photograph from light when not being viewed. The base and lid sit on a table or other surface.

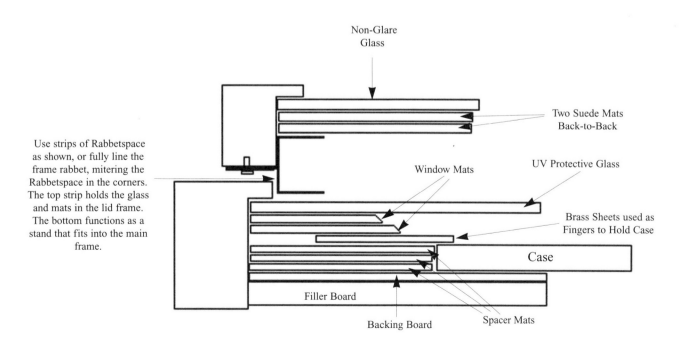

Framing Photography 77

Platform Easel

Project 13

This is an attractive display for any type of card photograph, but offers no protection from light. To make a UV glass cover, see project 5.

Paint the raw edges of the wood moulding before mounting to glass.

Use silicone to adhere the easel to the glass.

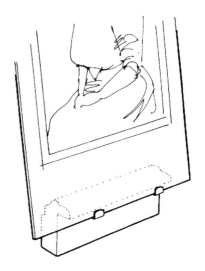

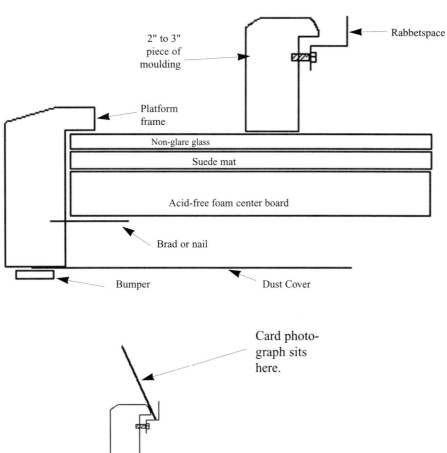

Float Mounting a Card Photograph

Project 14A

A float mount provides invisible support and allows all of the card photograph to show.

Cut the window mats with an opening that will give the card photograph ample area in which to be suspended.

A V-hinge should give sufficient support, especially for a card in very good condition, but an S-hinge can be useful for stronger support of cards that show brittle deterioration. (See page 54 for illustrations of float hinges.)

Matboard: Crescent 1106.
All mats should be buffered cotton rag.

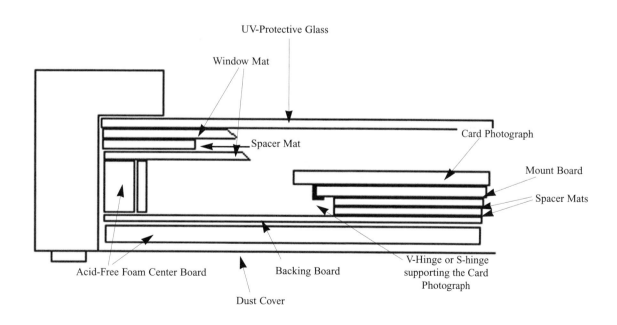

Framing Photography

Project 14B

This is another version of a float mount for a card photograph, using dark mat colors instead of pale neutrals. This looks especially good on photos mounted to dark colored cards, and photos with strong dark tones.

As with all card photographs, buffered rag matboards should be used wherever boards will touch the acidic card.

Mat Boards: Crescent 1562 & 1564

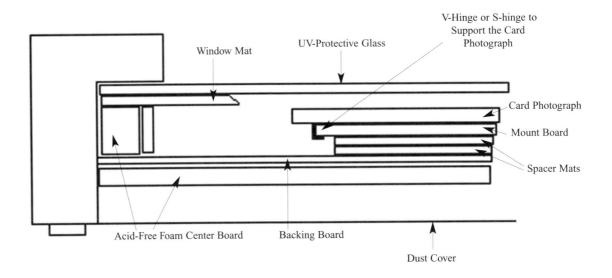

80 *Framing Photography*

Multiple Photographs

Project 15

If the photographs to be mounted are the only copies or have faded, it is best to copy the originals and frame the copies.

1. Dry mount photographs to non-buffered rag board.

2. Cut the photographs out of the mounting board. A bevel cut will create a line of white, black or color depending on the core color of the mounting board used. Or use a reverse bevel and no core will show.

3. Cut an oval opening in the back mat. Attach photo in opening with mounting strips or corners.

4. Place spacer mats under all the smaller photographs so that they float above the back mat. Some photographs should have more spacers under them to allow overlap. In this example, the rectangular photographs overlap. Use ATG tape to attach the layers together, and to attach each photo/spacer unit to the back mat.

Note: The photographs must not touch the glass, so the spacers in the rabbet of the frame must be at least one matboard thickness taller than the highest photo, or use framespace under the glass.

The spacers under each photograph should be 3/8" to 1/2" smaller than the photograph. If the spacers are too small, the photograph may warp; if too big, they may show. All spacers should be made of rag matboard.

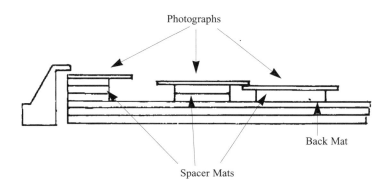

Framing Photography 81

Mounting a Photograph in a Shadowbox with a Three-dimensional Object

Project 16

1. Build the frame and cut the three mat openings.

2. Hinge or use corner mounts to attach the photograph and the certificate to the window mat.

3. If the medallion has a pin, use the pin to attach it to the backing. If not, sew the ribbon in place. Secure the pin or sewing stitches on the back of the board by inserting a small strip of rag matboard to prevent sagging.

4. Note the placement of the non-buffered rag in the drawing below. This is to protect the photograph. If the photograph is in color, having it copied and converted to a black and white print on fiber paper will greatly increase its life expectancy.

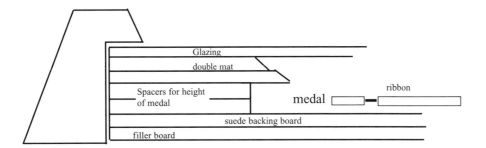

82 *Framing Photography*

CARD WITH OVAL PHOTO

Project 17

Some photo cards consist of an oval photograph mounted within an area of embossed oval designs. The design may be simply lines, or may be more decorative.

An oval window mat coordinates with the photo and allows the embossing to show. The rectangular top window mat provides comfortable breathing space within the design, without creating the distracting "target" look that can be caused by too many ovals-within-ovals.

Since the mats touch only the acidic card and not the photo, buffered matboards should be used throughout.

In the example here, the top mat is Crescent Moorman suede, the bottom mat is Crescent 1704. Both mats have spacer mats beneath them to achieve a shadow effect and more dimensional look.

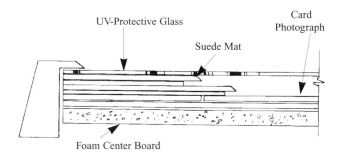

All other boards are Rag Mats

Framing Photography 83

Framing a Hand Oil-Colored Copy of an Early Photograph

Project 18

The original photograph was copied and printed onto a double-weight black and white fiber paper. The new copy has been oil-colored.

The oils must be completely dry before mounting and matting the photograph. A completely dry oil-colored photo may be dry mounted, but if not certain, use hinges instead.

Mat Boards: Crescent 1633 & 2298

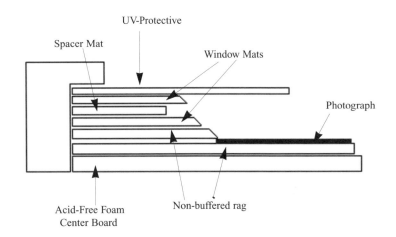

LARGE TINTYPE WITH ITS ORIGINAL MAT

Project 19

1. Make a double sink mat. The top sink mat is used to house and protect the original mat and the bottom sink mat supports the tintype. Since the old mat is acidic, buffered boards should be used for the top sink mat. The tintype emulsion is not made of animal protein, so buffered boards should also be used for the bottom sink mat.

2. Since the tintype is thin, use a two-ply rag spacer mat for tighter support. A rag spacer mat separates the two sink mats.

3. Since the old mat is quite brittle, add a top mat to protect the old mat from the glass and help support the edges.

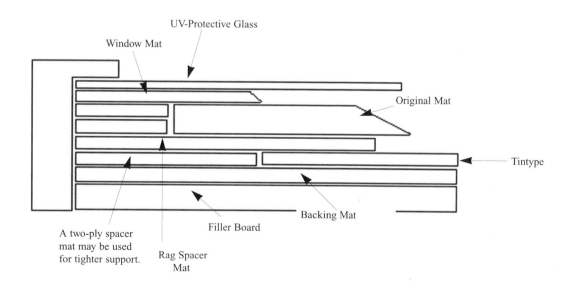

Framing Photography 85

Framing a Convex Print

Project 20

Convex prints are often brought into a frame shop without the original convex frame or glass, or with the glass broken. This method of framing a convex print offers an alternative to replacing the convex glass.

Handle these photographs carefully. No pressure should be placed on them. The old acidic mounting board will break easily if subjected to pressure or mishandling.

Since these photographs are mounted to acidic boards, the backing board used in framing must be buffered rag.

Cut an oval opening mat to cover the edges of the photograph, then place a spacer around the photo to support the mat, so that it does not actually rest on the photo. The oval mat, spacer, and backing board are attached to one another. The photograph is gently supported between the backing board and the oval mat.

Use shadowbox framing to build a case to contain the photograph.

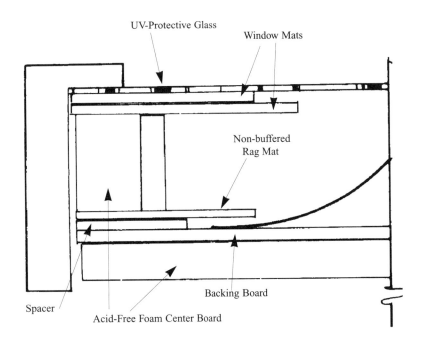

86 *Framing Photography*

Chapter 6
Frequently Asked Questions

Question: I have an old panoramic photo that was rolled up for years, and a smaller photo that is badly curled. Can I flatten them?
Answer: This is best left to a conservator, because of the great risk of cracking or breaking the print while flattening. This is especially true if the photograph has historic value, is a signed print, or is known to be done by a major photographer. However, for a customer's personal black and white, matte finish photos dated after 1890, with permission of the customer, a framer may use moisture methods to flatten. Do not use these methods on color photographs, glossy photos, or on photos from before 1890 (which are probably albumen prints).
METHOD A: Flattening in a dry mount press. Carefully moisten the photo by spraying a very fine mist of water on the back of the photograph. Sandwich the photo between two pieces of rag matboard, and place in the heated press (no more than 180 degrees F.) Open the press every 30-60 seconds to release steam, and to move the photo to a new location in the matboard sandwich (a drier area). Watch carefully for any softening of the emulsion. Work slowly and carefully. Decrease the time between press openings if any signs of sticking to the matboard are seen. If it is very tightly rolled set the leading edge into the press (between the boards) then slide in a small section at a time) Be very careful--brittle photos break! METHOD B: Passive moisture method, in which humidity gently enters the photo. Lay the print on a rack in an airtight container. Place a small amount of water in the bottom of the container, not touching the photograph. When the print relaxes, remove from the container, place between photo blotter papers, and dry under weight. Check frequently to make sure the emulsion is not sticking to the photo blotter paper.

Question: Are photographs safe in typical ready-made frames?
Answer: Most ready-made frames do not provide space between the photo and the glass. Over time, the emulsion may stick to the glass, and there is a very significant chance of losing them during separation. A spacer or mat should be placed in the frame to keep the photo from touching the glass. Also check the backing board provided. It is often an acidic cardboard which should be replaced with rag board.

Question: Can a photograph that has stuck to glass be removed without harm to the photo?
Answer: There are several methods that may work, but there will be some surface damage no matter which method is used. No method is guaranteed, so it is best to copy the photo before trying to save the original. METHOD A: Submerge the glass and photo in water, photo side up, glass side down, and wait for them to separate on their own. METHOD B: Apply dry ice or heat to the glass. The glass will shear itself from the photo.

Question: Can a convex photo that has split be repaired?
Answer: The careful application of mulberry tissue and wheat or rice starch paste can be used to repair the photograph. This will hold the pieces together, but the cracks in the emulsion will still show. Retouching dyes can sometimes be used to make the cracks less noticeable. This is not a conservation technique, but the owner of the photograph may opt for it to improve the appearance of the photo and allow it to be framed and hung for display. Always be careful with convex photographs. Their back boards are very acidic and brittle. They break easily under any pressure. See Project 20 on page 86 for framing.

Question: Can broken convex glass be replaced?
Answer: Convex glass is available in the original standard sizes, and can be custom made.

Question: Does copying harm the original photograph?
Answer: The short exposure to light during normal copying will not harm photographs.

Question: I had a color photo copied and the colors are different. What caused this?
Answer: There are several possible reasons. A) The wrong lighting was used for the copy film, causing the final print to appear warmer or colder than the original. B) The chemistry is exhausted. C) The filter pack used in the enlarger was wrong. A black and white copy print is usually not quite as good as the original due to focus loss and contrast shift. A color copy has the additional problem of color shift.

Question: Can a color photo be copied as a black and white print?
Answer: Yes, it can be copied onto a black and white negative and printed on appropriate paper. If the color image is on a negative it also can be printed in black and white. The most stable paper is a fiber photographic paper. If the photo lab uses color paper it will not last as long as a black and white fiber print by many years. Toning can produce a very nice brown or sepia shading to a black and white print.

Question: Can a color photo be made from a black and white print?
Answer: It can be copied and oil colored. This is the traditional method and samples of this process have lasted over a hundred years. Another method is to scan the black and white into a computer and add color to the image, then print as a color print. A color print will not last as long as an oil colored print.

Framing Photography 87

APPENDIX

Photographic Sizes

The following sizes are published sizes of various photographic products from the past through to the present. The image being measured may not conform with the sizes stated because of expansion or contraction of the board or slight differences in production sizes.

Sizes of Early Glass, Mounts, Paper, Daguerreotypes, Etc.

One sixteenth plate	1-5/8x1-3/8"
Petite cards	1-5/8x3-1/8"
One-ninth plate	2x2-1/2"
One-sixth plate	3-3/4x3-1/4"
One-fourth plate	
(Quarter plate)	3-1/4x4-1/4"
(Dry plate process only)	4x5"
Double quarter plate	4-1/4x6-1/2"
Half plate (usual)	4-3/4x6-1/2"
(Dry plate process only)	5x7"
Whole plate (4-4)	6-1/2x8-1/2"
Extra 4-4	8x10"

Sizes of Mounts

Stereoscopic	1859*	3x5", 3-1/2x7", 4x7", 4-1/4x7", 4-1/2x7", 5x7", 5x8"
Boudoir		5-1/4x8-1/2"
Cabinet	1866*	4-1/4x6-1/2", 4-1/2x6-1/2"
Carte-de-visite	1859*	2-1/2x4-1/8", 2-1/2x4-1/4", 2-1/2x3-7/8", 2-1/2x4"
Imperial		7-7/8x9-7/8", 6-7/8x9-7/8"
Minette		1-1/2x2-3/8"
Panel		4x8-1/4"
Promenade	1875*	4-1/8x7-1/8", 4x7"
Victoria	1870*	3-1/4x5"

* the year it was introduced to the United States

Modern Photographic Sizes

These are standard sheet sizes, other sizes are possible by cutting down a standard

4x5"	11x14"
5x7"	16x20"
8x10"	20x24"
8-1/2x11"	

Square Format

5x5"
8x8"
10x10"

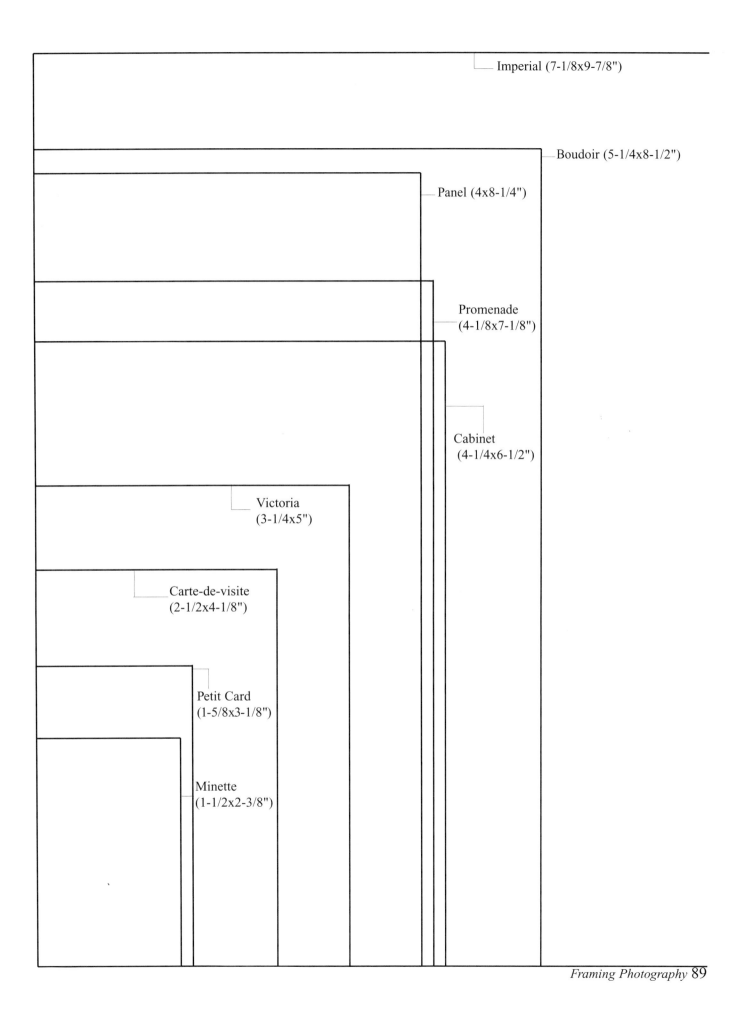

Framing Photography 89

Glossary

ALBUMEN (albumin). Dried egg white used primarily in the preparation of printing paper binder from about 1850. It was replaced by gelatin in the 1880s. Albumen was also used as a binder for glass plates and was used to produce fine quality lantern slides.

ALBUMENISED PAPER (ALBUMEN PAPER). Paper which has a coating made of salt and albumen.

ALKALI. A chemical compound with a pH greater than 7. Solutions that are alkaline usually feel slippery or soapy to the touch and are difficult to wash off. Alkali chemicals used in color chemistry are very damaging to the eyes and skin.

BARYTA PAPER. Paper which has an emulsion coating of sulphate of barium. Used for a layer between the emulsion and the paper substrate. Provides a smoother and whiter surface.

BASE. 1.The film or print substrate (acetate, polyester, glass, paper, etc.) which is coated with a photographic emulsion. 2. Having properties similar to those of an alkali. Being able to react with acids to produce salts. Also "basic".

BICHROMATE. More recently known as DICHROMATE. Light-sensitive alkaline bichromates, such as the chromium salts of sodium, potassium, and ammonium, which are used in the gum and oil pigment printing processes. Very poisonous.

BINDER. Chemical layer that holds the silver particles suspended in an evenly distributed manner. Some of the more successful commercial binders are albumen, gelatin and collodion.

BLACK BORDERS. The edge around the image in a print. Normally, this border is white, which means no exposure. The border is caused by the leaves of the print easel that hold the paper during exposure. Black borders mean that the print had to be fogged with light before or after image exposure with the image area covered up. Can produce very dramatic photographic style.

BROMIDE PRINT PAPER. Paper with an emulsion consisting of bromide of silver in gelatin which may or may not include other silver haloids. This paper was used in developing when contact printing or enlarging with artificial light or daylight. The introduction of bromide paper retired albumen print paper.

BROWN TONING. The use of a brown toner solution in a final bath after a complete washing has been accomplished. See TONING. When brown toning a silver gelatin print, it will turn a warm, almost reddish-brown.

BUFFER. A chemical solution that has been designed to hold a chemical pH at a certain prescribed level. Pertaining to framing, the calcium carbonate added to matboard acts as a buffer to keep the pH of the mat at about 8.3, or on the alkaline end of the pH scale.

CARBRO PROCESS. See OZOBROME process.

COMPLETION. A term used by a photographer to indicate the chemical reaction is finished. In the case of some emulsions, such as albumen prints, the completion of the chemical reaction is not finished until the image has disappeared.

CONCAVE. Hollowed or curved inward. The opposite of convex.

CONTACT PAPER. Printing paper designed to be clamped against a negative and exposed in a print frame. The resulting print is the exact same size or 1:1 as the negative. Contact paper can be either developing- or printing-out paper. As a developing out paper, it is usually slower than the normal projection printing paper used with an enlarger. This is used for producing contact prints for filing and selection of negatives for final printing.

CONTRAST. The difference in image density from white to black. Low contrast usually means most of the image is light and dark grays. High contrast means that there are mostly pure whites and blacks with few grays.

CONVEX PRINT. A print which bulges outward that is mounted onto pulp board and is found in oval, rectangle and multiple-sided formats.

CROP. The term is used to describe the process of eliminating part of the image that is on the negative during the printing step.

DENSE. The term refers to the thickness of the silver image. A dense image on a negative means that the silver is very thick and difficult to print.

DENSITY. The opacity of the photographic image.

DEVELOPING-OUT. A term used to differentiate between the chemical development of a print and the printing-out or physical development of the print.

DRY MOUNTING PRESS. The heat press that is used in the dry mount process. A dry mounting press may have a soft bed or a hard bed. Normal dry mounting is usually done with the soft bed press or the heated vacuum press. The hard bed press is used more in the laminating process.

DRY MOUNTING TISSUE. The heat-activated adhesive used in the dry mounting process. There are two basic types: the type that bonds as it is heated and the type that bonds as it cools. The one that bonds as it cools can be reversed, but it does not meet conservation standards since there are traces of the adhesive left after separation.

EMULSION. The light-sensitive chemical which is coated onto film or paper to produce a negative, positive or print. Usually made of animal protein gelatin which is coated onto film or paper.

ENLARGER. Originally developed from the solar camera, this was invented in the 1850s and used the sun or daylight to provide the needed light for the exposure of the print material. Later, the enlarger was developed and was designed to use artificial light produced from electricity and oil or gas. Today, most enlargers are designed to expose paper laying flat in an easel on the bench top.

ENLARGING. The act of making an image on a negative larger during the printing process by using an enlarger.

EXPOSURE. Placing a photographic emulsion under light combined with the total amount of light that is allowed to hit the emulsion.

f./64 GROUP. A group of dedicated photographers including: Ansel Easton Adams, Imogen Cunningham and Edward Weston. This group aspired for the sharpest image possible, much in opposition to the earlier Photo-Secessionists or Linked Ring group. They used large format cameras stopped down to the smallest aperture and normally made contact prints. This resulted in everything being in focus and no grain showing due to enlargement. The group was started in the early 1930s.

FADING. 1. Fading of Negatives. This is due to insufficient washing or fixing, and the consequent action of hypo (see SODIUM HYPOSULPHITE) on the delicate image or silver. 2. Fading of Prints. Caused in most cases by sulphur or its compounds.

FILM, PHOTOGRAPHIC. A thin, clear flexible sheet of plastic which is coated on one side with a gelatin made of light-sensitive silver compounds.

GLOSSY. The term used for photographic prints that are finished with a very reflective surface that is smooth like glass.

GOLD TONING. See TONING.

GRAIN. Developed silver collects in clumps and appears to be grain when the image is enlarged. Usually the faster films are more grainy than slower ones.

GUM ARABIC. A water soluble gum used to manufacture adhesives.

HARSH. Very high contrast that is not pleasant to the eye.

HELIOGRAPHY. The first successful photographic process invented in the 1820s by Joseph Nicephore Niepce.

HIGHLIGHTS. The lightest areas of the subject when seen in a photographic print.

LATENT IMAGE. The invisible photographic image that is recorded on the emulsion during exposure.

MASKING. Blocking out portions of a photograph.

MATTE. A non-glossy surface which is achieved with the use of special paper surfaces or by a lack of ferrotyping the print while it is drying.

NEGATIVE. An image with the lights and shades reversed, usually on film or glass.

OPAQUE. Inability to transmit light.

OVEREXPOSED. When an emulsion is exposed to too much light and the film is developed, the image will be blocked up in the highlight areas.

RC PAPERS. Resin-coated paper designed to allow machine processing. The coating seals the paper fibers so that chemicals are easy to wash off the paper.

REGISTER. The lines and shapes must match each other to produce a good sharp image.

RESIN-COATED PAPERS. See RC PAPER.

RESOLUTION. The ability of a lens to separate shapes from one another. A resolution chart is sometimes made of lines or rectangle shapes. The higher the resolution, the sharper focus the lens.

SENSITIVITY. The ability of a material to respond to light.

SEPARATION. 1. The differentiation between light and dark shapes or between the background and the subject matter. 2. Special black and white negatives that are used to record each of the primary color images of a subject. These separation negatives are then used to print color images such as in the tri-color carbon process or the dye transfer process.

SEPIA TONING. A sulfide toner that produces a brown or sepia tone on the processed photographic print.

SLIDE. A modern version of the lantern slide. A term used for the 35mm color slide.

SLOW. A rating of a photographic emulsion's sensitivity to light. The emulsion is somewhat insensitive to light.

SOFT. A term used to mean a sightly out of focus image. Often used as a term to describe portraiture lenses.

STAIN. A discoloration caused in an emulsion by exhausted developer, poor fixation or poor washing and/or contamination. A stain usually is not stable and advanced staining will continue over time.

STEREOSCOPE. A device used to view a stereograph (stereogram) in 3-D.

TACKING IRON. A small electric heating iron that is used in the dry mounting process. Used to provide a small spot of heat which activates the dry mounting adhesive in order to temporarily hold the art or photograph to the substrate while it is being prepared for the dry mount press.

THIN. A term used to describe a underexposed or underdeveloped negative.

TIPPED IN. A method of attaching art or photographs into a book with the use of glue.

TONING. A chemical bath used to convert the silver image to a different color or increase its life expectancy. Some of the more popular toners were gold, platinum, selenium, sepia, and brown toners. The toner converted some of the silver image to a different metal or a sulfide.

WASHED OUT. Used to describe the results of an overexposed negative. The image will have little detail and will be very light in density.

BIBLIOGRAPHY

Arnow, Jan. *Handbook of Alternative Photographic Processes.* New York: Van Nostrand Reinhold Company, 1982

Aver, Michel. *The Illustrated History of the Camera.* Boston: New York Graphic Society, 1975.

Brettall, Richard R. *Paper and Light, The Calotype in Frame and Great Britain.* Boston: David R. Godine, 1984.

Bunnell, Peter C. *A Photographic Vision, Pictoral Photography.* Peregrine Smith, Inc, 1980

Davis, Phil. *Photography.* New York: Mayflower Books, Inc., 1979.

Dennis, Landt and Lisl Dennis. *Collecting Photographs.* New York: E.P. Dutton, 1977.

Doty, Robert. *Photo-Secession.* Rochester: George Eastman House, Inc., 1978.

Doty, Robert. *Photography in America.* New York: Random House, 1974.

Gernsheim, Helmut and Alison Gernsheim. *A Concise History of Photography.* London: Thames and Hudson, 1971.

Haist, Grant. Modern *Photographic Processing Vol. 1,* New York: John Wiley and Sons, 1979.

Hartmann, Sadakichi. The Valiant Knights of Daguerre. Berkeley: University of California Press, 1978.

Haworth-Booth, Mark. *The Golden Age of British Photography.* Millerton: Aperture, 1984.

Keefe Jr., Laurence, E., and Dennis Inch. *The Life of a Photograph.* Woburn: Butterworth Publishers, 1984.

Kodak Photographic Products Group. *Conservation of Photographs.* Rochester: Eastman Kodak Company, 1985.

Lucie-Smith, Edward. *The Invented Eye.* New York: Two Continents Publishing Group, 1975.

Mace, O. Henry. *Collector's Guide to Early Photographs.* Radnor: Wallace-Homestead Book Company, 1990.

Martin, Judy and Annie Colbeck. *Handtinting Photographs.* Oxfordshire: Amanuensis Books Limited, 1989.

Mathews, Oliver. *Early Photographs and Early Photographers.* London: Reedminster Publications Ltd., 1973.

Mitchell, Margaretta K. *Recollection – Ten Women of Photography.* New York: The Viking Press, 1979.

Nadeau, Luis. *Gum Dichromate and Other Direct Carbon Processes From Artgue to Zimmerman.* Fredericton: Atelier, 1987.

Nadeau, Luis. *History and Practice of Oil and Bromoil Printing.* Fredericton: Atelier, 1985.

Newhall, Beaumont, and Nancy Newhall. *Masters of Photography.* New York: George Braziller, Inc.

Pfister, Harold Francis, *Facing the Light.* Washington D.C.: Smithsonian Institution Press, 1978.

Pollack, Peter. *The Picture History of Photography.* New York: Harry N. Abrams.

Reilly, James M. *Care and Identification of 19th Century Photographic Prints.* Rochester: Eastman Kodak Company, 1986.

Reilly, James M. "Image Deterioration in Albumen Photographic Prints" *Science and Technology in the Service of Conservation, 3-9 September 1982.* N. S. Brommelle and Gary Thompson, eds. (London I.I. C. 1982).

Reilly, James M. "Role of the Mailard, or 'Protein-Sugar' Reaction in Highlight Yellowing of Albumen Photographic Prints" *Preprints, 10th Annual Meeting Milwaukee, Wisconsin 26-30 May 1982.* (Milwaukee: A.I.C. 1982).

Rempel, Siegfried. T*he Care of Photographs.* New York: Lyons and Burford Publishers, 1987.

Sandler, Martin W. *The Story of American Photography.* Boston: Little, Brown and Company, 1979

Stieglitz, Alfred. *Camera Work A Pictorial Guide.* New York: Dover Publications, 1978.

Taft, Robert. *Photography and the American Scene.* New York: Dover Publications, 1938.

Time Life Books. *The Print.* Alexandria: Time Life Books, 1981.

Thomas, D.B., *The Science Museum Photography Collection.* London: Her Majesty's Stationary Office.

Travis, David. *Photography Rediscovered, American Photographs, 1900-1930.* New York: Whitney Museum of American Art, 1979.

Wall, E.J. *Dictionary of Photography.* London: Harell, Watson and Viney, 1902.

Wilhelm, Henry, and Carol Brower. *The Permanence and Care of Color Photographs.* Grinnell: Preservation Publishing Company, 1993.

Wills, Camfield, and Deirdre Wills. *History of Photography.* London: The Hamlyn Publishing Company, 1980.

INDEX

italicized page numbers reference pictures of photographs

A
Adams, Ansel 11, 44, 46, 91
Adamson, Robert 25, 45
albumen 10-11, *12-13*, 14-15, *18-19*, 20-22, *21-22*, 39, 44, 51-52, 56, 90
albumen paper 11, 21, 90
albums 12
Agfa 27
ambrotype 10-11, *12*, 14, *18-19*, 23-24, *23-24*, 70, 73, 76
Archer, Frederick Scott 10, 23

B
Bayard, Hippolyte 25
Berger, Charles 48
blueprint process *see* cyanotype
boudoir card 15, 22, 40, 46, 88, *89*
Brady, Matthew 22
Braun, Adolph 26

C
Calotype 10, 12, *18-19*, 14, 25, 45
cabinet card 11, 15, *15*, 16, 22, 40, 46, 90
Cameron, Julia Margaret 22
carbon print *12*, *18-19*, 26
carte-de-visite 11, 14, *15*, 16, 22, 40, 46, 47, 49, 56, 71, *71*, 88, *89*, 90
Cibachrome *see* Ilfochrome Classic
Coburn, Alvin Langdon 37, 42, 43
computer generated images 28-29, *57*
conservation framing, for photography 49
    boards, buffering 50
    considerations 49
    cotton 51
    lignin 51
    paper 50
    see also corner mounts, edge mounts, hinges, pocket and suspenders, s-hinge, sink mats, t-hinge, v-hinge, and z-hinge
convex print 86, *86*, 90
corner mounts 16, 55
Curtis, Edward S. 42
crayon print 11, *12*, *18-19*, 30, *30*
cyanotype 10, *12-13*, *18-19*, 20, 31, *31*, 51

D
Daguerre, Louis Jacques Mande 10, 32
daguerreotype 10-11, *12*, 14, *18-19*, 23, 25 ,32-33, *32,* 70, 73, 76, 88
Demachy, Robert 37, 41
digital 35
dry mounting 20, 57-58, 84
    recommendations for *57*
dye sublimation 28,29
dye transfer *13*, *18-19*, 20, 34, 51, 92

E
edge mounts 55
Ektacolor 27
Emerson, P.H. 43
enlarger 10, 30, 90, 91 *see also* solar camera
Eugene, Frank 37
Evans, Frederick H. 43
EverColor *13*, *18-19*, 35

F
f./64 Group 11, 91
Frith, Frances 22
Fujicolor 27

G
gaslight paper *12-13*, *18-19*, 36, *36*
glass, detaching photos from 87
gum bichromate (gum dichromate) *12-13*, *18-19*, 37, *37*

H
hand-tinted print 24, 32, 46, 47
heliography *12*, 91
Herschel, Sir John 10, 31
Hill, David Octavius 25, 45
Hill, Robert 25
hinges 52-54
    pockets and suspenders 52
    s-hinge 54
    t-hinge 53
    v-hinge 54
    z-hinge 54
Huston, William 26

I
Ilfochrome Classic *13*, *18-19*, 38, *38*, 51, 57
imperial card 15, 22, 40, 46, 88, *89*
ink jet print 28, *28* 29, *29*
Iris printer 29
ivorytype *12-13*, *18-19*, 39, *39*

K
Kodacolor 13, 18-19, 27
Konica 27
Kuhns, W.J. 26

L
Langenheim, F. 45
Langenheim, W. 45
laser prints 29
le Secq, Henri 45
Levitt, Helen 46
Linked Ring movement 11, 91

M
matt collodion *12-13*, *18-19*, 40, *40*
minette card 15, 22, 40, 40, 46, 88, *89*
Moroccan case 14, *14*, 24, 70, 73
mounting boards 17
Muybridge, Eadweard 22

N
Newhall, Beaumont 46
Niepce, Nicephore 10, 91
Niepce de Saint-Victor, Abel 10

O
oil pigment *12-13*, *18-19*, 41, *41*, 90
orange peel 38, 64

P
panel card 15, 22, 40, 40, 46, 88, *89*
paper folder 12, 46, 65
photographic albums 12
    cardboard 12
    cloth 12
    leather 12
    magnetic 12
    paper bound 12
photogravure *12-13*, *18-19*, 42
platinum print (platinotype) 11, *12-13*, *18-19*, 43, *43*
pockets and suspenders 52
Polaroid *13*, *18-19*, 44, *44*, 57, *57*
pressure-sensitive mounting 60-61
printing-out paper (P.O.P) *18-19*, 40
promenade card 15, 22, 40, 46, 88, *89*

R
RC paper 27, 46, 92
resin-coated material 13 *see also* RC paper

S
s-hinge 54
salted paper print *12*, 15, *18-19*, 45, *45*
silver developing-out gelatin print *18-19*, 46, *46*
silver developing-out paper *12*
sink mat 56
solar camera 10, 30, 91 *see also* enlarger
spray coating 16
spray mounting 63
static mounting 64
stereograph (stereo card) 15, 22, 40, 46, 88
stereoscope 92
Steichen, Edward 11, 42-43, 46
Stieglitz, Alfred 11, 42, 43, 46
Strand, Paul 42

T
t-hinge 53
Talbot, Fox 45
Talbot, William Henry 10, 25
Talbotype 10, 25 *see also* Calotype
tintype 9-11, *12-13*, 14, *15*, 16, 47, 70, 73, 76, 79, 85, *85*
tools, for identification 9

U
UltraStable *13*, *18-19*, 48
Union case 14, *14*, 24, 33

V
v-hinge 54
Victoria card 15, 22, 40, 46, 88, *89*

W
Weston, Edward 11, 91
wet collodion process (wet plate) 10-11, *18-19*, 23, 47, *47*
wet mounting 62
Whistler, John 25
White, Clarence 11, 37, 42, 43

Z
z-hinge 54
z-tack 58

Framing Photography

• • • • • BOOKS • • • • •

THE LIBRARY OF PROFESSIONAL PICTURE FRAMING

Picture Framing Vol 1 by Vivian Kistler CPF, GCF
The best book on Framing! History of Framing • How to chose Moulding • How to place orders • Equipment • Cutting & Joining Moulding • Cutting Glass & Plastics • Designing a custom frame job. • Measuring • Mat Cutting • Stretching Canvas and Fabrics • Conservation • Work Orders • Floorplans
    96pp   8-1/2 x 11   B116 $19

Mat Cutting & Decoration Vol 2 by Vivian Kistler CPF, GCF
Inlays, Offsets, Doubles & 8-sided mats! Step-by-step directions for 50 different mats, basic to advanced. Measurements • Proportion • Color • Fractions • Faux Finishes • Hand-cut designs • Singles • Doubles • Multiple Openings • V-grooves • French Mats • Cove & Fabric-wrapped Mats
    96pp   8-1/2 x 11   B019 $19

Framing Needlework & Fabric Vol 3 by Vivian Kistler CPF, GCF
Block & Stretch Needlepoint • 12 Methods of Mounting Textiles • 15 Projects • Types of Needlework & Fabric • Notions • Cleaning • Repairs • Pressing. Learn to frame crewel, needlepoint, cross-stitch, antique samplers, quilts, scarves, kimonos, carpets, scrolls, hankies, doilies, Persian paintings, papyrus, weavings & flags.
    96pp   8-1/2 x 11   B027 $19

Conservation Framing Vol 4 by Vivian C. Kistler, CPF, GCF
Handling Art on Paper • Glazing • Hinges & support methods • Adhesives • Types of Boards • Encapsulation • Deacidification • Problems & Solutions • Projects • Framing watercolors, pastels, papyrus, photos, skin documents • techniques for broken and brittle artwork. Cleaning and repairs.
    96pp   8-1/2x11   B035 $19

Mounting Methods Vol 5 by Vivian C. Kistler, CPF, GCF
Dry • Wet • Spray • Pressure-Sensitives • Sprays Adhesives • Types of Mounting Boards • Buckling Workstations • Mounting Basics • Equipment Laminating • Canvas Transfer • Step-by-Step Projects
    96pp   8-1/2x11   B043 $19

The Articles of Business   by Vivian Kistler CPF
16 chapters on the business of operating a frame shop and gallery. Volume Framing • Credit Departments • Pricing • Employee Productivity • Leasing • Corporate Sales • Marketing • Advertising • Financial Statements, Credit Terms, and more. Over 100 answers to questions sent to the "Ask the Expert"
    192pp   6 x 9   B280 $20

Color & Design for the Picture Framer by Nona Powers CPF
Learn how to select the size, color and shape of mats, mouldings and decorative elements. See the relationship of color and size, of warm and cool colors and moulding color to mat color. Full-color artworks with different matting selections. Learn to design a professional framed presentation. A workbook with practice sheets are included in the back of the book. This book is the basis for Nona's popular two-day course she has been teaching for the PPFA and distributors for many years.
    80pp   8-1/2x11   B485 $20

How to Build Frameshop Worktables, Fixtures & Jigs
    by Paul MacFarland CPF
Building plans for 25 projects. Build a Frame Rack • Frame Jack • Support for Length Moulding • Spool Wire Box • Table for your Mat Cutter • Roll Storage • Bin Cart & more! Materials, Tools & Techniques. Table, tops, cabinets, clamps, storage for mat, glass, moulding & customer's goods.
    64pp   8-1/2 x 11   B361 $19

Brian Wolf's Fantasy Finishes for Mat Decoration
Brian shares the secrets of his subtle & elegantly decorated mats. Marble metallic & sandstone finish panels. Learn how to create your own fantasy finishes, using powders, paints and inks. Brian's special color recipes! How to use ruling pens.
    64pp   8-1/2 x 11   B337 $19

Business Forms for Galleries & Frame Shops
by Vivian Kistler CPF
Consignment Record & Agreement • Work Orders • Sales Records • Projected Sales Charts • Record of Condition of Artwork • Purchase Orders • Time Sheets • Tax Exempt Slips • Petty Cash Slips • Commission Forms • Proposal • Inventory • Yearly Planner • Sales Tracking & More! Ready to copy.
    32pp   8-1/2 x 11   B264 $12

Floorplans for Galleries & Frame Shops
Maximize your space! 19 floorplans • Equipment • Lighting • Flooring • Storage • Safety. Front & backroom plans for shops from 400 to 4,000 sq.ft. Grid paper included, plus furniture & equipment patterns!
    32pp   8-1/2 x 11   B272 $14

How To Do Object Box Framing   by V. Kistler
Support & attach items in a shadow box. 20 different projects. Attachments, backgrounds & special requirements for problem pieces. Coins • Plates • Fossils • Animals • Ceramics • Jewelry • Flowers • Figurines • Buttons • Masks • Clothing
    32pp   8-1/2 x 11   B345 $14

Decorative Accessories Made From Moulding
Ever wonder what to do with all those pieces of scrap moulding? Learn how to transform them into imaginative creations! What To Make • How To Measure • Cutting • Building • Lining • Finishing Tips. Step-By-Step Instructions for Building Dozens of Projects. • Clocks • Boxes • Tray • Wall Shelf • Sconces • Humidor • Mirrors • Jewelry Box • Business Card Holder • Bulletin Board • Three-panel Screen • Curio Cabinet • Architectural Elements • Many More!
    32pp   8-1/2 x 11   B604 $16

• • VIDEO WORKSHOPS • •

KISTLER'S ALL NEW VIDEOS FOR 1999

The Basics of Picture Framing
by Vivian Kistler CPF
Basic training for picture framers & designers! Step-by-step instructions. Moulding • Squaring a Mat Cutter • Cutting Single & Double Mats • Color Selection • Matboards • Measuring • Cutting Glass • Framing Needlework • Stretching Paintings • Fitting • Attaching Artwork • Dust Cover • Screw Eyes & Wire
    60 min   VHS   V132 $30

Mat Cutting & Decoration
by Vivian Kistler CPF
Designing and using color mats. Step-by-step instructions for cutting single, double, inlay & V-groove mats. Cutting & decorating techniques. Fabric-wrapped, shadow-box, traditional French mats, and application of marbled papers. Conservation. Attaching Artwork. Matting needlework & 3-D objects.
    60 min   VHS   V140 $30

Conservation Framing of Paper Art
How to make hinges. How to preserve newsprint paper & boards. Neutral pH. How to de-acidify & encapsulate art on paper. How to choose boards, tapes, adhesives & glazing. Hinges • Flanges • Mounting Strips • Pockets • Float & Sink Mats
    60 min   VHS   V175 $30

Framing Needlework & Fabric
by Vivian Kistler CPF, GCF
Block & Stretch needlepoint. Frame any type of fabric or stitched piece. Types, supplies & materials. Blocking, stretching, matting & framing. Projects include sweaters, doilies, Chinese embroidery, large scarves, cross-stitch, crewel & needlepoint, Persian paintings, Kalangas, Molas & sheer fabrics. Conservation. Lacing, pinning, stapling & sewing.
    60 min   VHS   V167 $30

Designing Custom Framing
by Vivian Kistler CPF
Learn the Rules of Thumb of frame design. How to choose mat colors and coordinating frames. Color and proportion; how to select the size of mats and frames and placement of multiple openings. How to handle black & white pictures, old photos, mixed sizes, mismatched art. See how different color mats change the mood of a picture.
    60 min   VHS   V191 $30

THE BRIAN WOLF MAT DECORATION SERIES

The Art of Ink Lines   by Brian Wolf CPF
Brian shows you in exacting detail the techniques of perfect lines on mats. How to draw consistent ink lines • Laying out lines • How to use lines as an accent on inlays • Drawing lines on circles and ovals • Lining offset corners • Coordinating multiple lines • How to use a ruling pen.
    30 min   VHS   V40X $20

Painted Mat Decoration   by Brian Wolf CPF
Brian demonstrates the step-by-step process of painting faux panels. Unique recipes for marbleizing & faux finishes. Brian shows you several methods of making panels by masking, stencil, powder resist, and glazing. Gold, malachite & metallic recipes.
    30 min   VHS   V426 $20

Hand Carved Mats   by Brian Wolf CPF
Brian demonstrates his award-winning carving skills. The tools and techniques are thoroughly explained and demonstrated. Subtle, carved designs accent mats and create an elegant balance. How to add top & bottom ornaments and partial grooves.
    30 min   VHS   V418 $20

Marbled Paper Panels & Bevels   by Brian Wolf CPF
Learn to create extraordinary mats with marbled papers. Panels, unique corners and overlays. Bevels: thick, thin painted and wrapped. Brian uses stunning papers in innovative ways!
    30 min   VHS   V442 $20

*Order these books and videos from
frame supply distributors or contact:*

COLUMBA PUBLISHING CO. INC.,
330 836-2619 • Fax 330 836-9659 • 800 999-7491
2003 W. Market St. • Akron, OH 44313 USA
www.columbapublishing.com